Karen Morrison and Lucille Dunne

Cambridge IGCSE®

Mathematics

Core Practice Book

Second edition

CAMBRIDGE
UNIVERSITY PRESS

CAMBRIDGE
UNIVERSITY PRESS

University Printing House, Cambridge CB2 8BS, United Kingdom

One Liberty Plaza, 20th Floor, New York, NY 10006, USA

477 Williamstown Road, Port Melbourne, VIC 3207, Australia

314–321, 3rd Floor, Plot 3, Splendor Forum, Jasola District Centre, New Delhi – 110025, India

79 Anson Road, 06–04/06, Singapore 079906

Cambridge University Press is part of the University of Cambridge.

It furthers the University's mission by disseminating knowledge in the pursuit of education, learning and research at the highest international levels of excellence.

www.cambridge.org
Information on this title: www.cambridge.org/9781108437226

© Cambridge University Press 2018

First edition 2012
Second edition 2018

20 19 18 17 16 15 14 13 12 11 10 9 8 7 6 5 4

Printed in Spain by GraphyCems

A catalogue record for this publication is available from the British Library

ISBN 978-1-108-43722-6 Paperback

Cover image: eugenesergeev/Getty images

Contents

Introduction

This highly illustrated practice book has been written by experienced teachers to help students revise the *Cambridge IGCSE® Mathematics* (0580/0980) Core syllabuses. Packed full of exercises, the only narrative consists of helpful bulleted lists of key reminders and useful advice in the margins for anyone needing more support.

There is plenty of practice offered via 'drill' exercises throughout each chapter. These consist of progressive and repetitive questions that allow you to practise methods applicable to each subtopic. At the end of each chapter there are 'Mixed exercises' that bring together all the subtopics of a chapter in such a way that you have to decide for yourself what methods to use. The answers to *all* of these questions are supplied at the back of the book. This should encourage you to assess your progress as you go along, choosing to do more or less practice as required.

The book has been written with a clear progression from start to finish, with some later chapters requiring knowledge learned in earlier chapters. There are useful signposts throughout that link the content of the chapters, allowing you to follow your own course through the book: where the content in one chapter might require knowledge from a previous chapter, a comment is included in a 'Rewind' box; and where content will be practised in more detail later on, a comment is included in a 'Fast forward' box. Examples of both are included below:

◀ REWIND

You learned how to plot lines from equations in chapter 10. ◀

FAST FORWARD ▶

You will learn much more about sets in chapter 9. For now, just think of a set as a list of numbers or other items that are often placed inside curly brackets. ▶

Other helpful guides in the margin of the book are as follows:

Clues: these light grey boxes contain general comments to remind you of important or key information that is useful when tackling an exercise, or simply useful to know. They often provide extra information or support in potentially tricky topics.

Remember, when working with right-angled triangles you may still need to use Pythagoras.

Tip: these are tips that relate to good practice in answering questions in mathematics. They cover common pitfalls based on the authors' experiences of their students, and point you to things to be wary of or to remember in order to be successful with your studies.

! Tip

It is essential that you remember to work out *both* unknowns. Every pair of simultaneous linear equations will have a pair of solutions.

Problem-solving: as you work through the course, you will develop your own 'toolbox' of problem-solving skills and strategies. These darker grey boxes will remind you of the problem-solving framework and suggest ways of tackling different types of problems.

The *Core Practice Book* mirrors the chapters and subtopics of the *Cambridge IGCSE® Mathematics Core and Extended Coursebook Second edition* written by Karen Morrison and Nick Hamshaw. However, this book has been written such that it can be used without this coursebook; it can be used as a revision tool by any student regardless of what coursebook they are using.

Read these problems carefully so that you will be able to recognise similar problems in future, even if you are not told to use HCF and LCM.

Also in the *Cambridge IGCSE® Mathematics* series:

Cambridge IGCSE® Mathematics Core and Extended Coursebook (9781108437189)

Cambridge IGCSE® Mathematics Core and Extended Coursebook with Cambridge Online Mathematics (2 years) (9781108525732)

Cambridge IGCSE® Mathematics Extended Practice Book (9781108437219)

Cambridge IGCSE® Mathematics Teacher's Resource (9781108701532)

Cambridge IGCSE® Mathematics Revision Guide (9781108437264)

1 Reviewing number concepts

1.1 Different types of numbers

- Real numbers can be divided into rational and irrational numbers. You will deal with rational numbers in this chapter. Irrational numbers are covered in chapter 9.
- Rational numbers can be written as fractions in the form of $\frac{a}{b}$ where a and b are integers and $b \neq 0$. (Integers are negative and positive whole numbers, and zero.)
- Integers, fractions and terminating decimals are all rational numbers.

Tip
Make sure you know what the following sets of numbers are: natural numbers, integers, odd and even numbers and prime numbers.

Knowing the correct mathematical terms is important for understanding questions and communicating mathematically.

Exercise 1.1

1 Copy and complete this table by writing a definition and giving an example of each type of number.

Mathematical name	Definition	Example
Natural numbers		
Integers		
Prime numbers		
Square numbers		
Fraction		
Decimal		

2 Include numbers to show what each of the following symbols means. For example $100 > 99$.

   a $>$ b $\leqslant$ c $\approx$ d $\therefore$
   e $\sqrt{}$ f $\neq$ g $\geqslant$ h $<$

3 Look at this set of numbers.

   $3, -2, 0, 1, 9, 15, 4, 5, -7, 10, 32, -32, 21, 23, 25, 27, 29, \frac{1}{2}$

   a Which of these numbers are NOT natural numbers?
   b Which of these numbers are NOT integers?
   c Which of these numbers are prime numbers?
   d Which of these numbers are square numbers?

4 List:

   a four square numbers greater than 100.
   b four rational numbers smaller than $\frac{1}{3}$.
   c two prime numbers that are > 80.
   d the prime numbers < 10.

1.2   Multiples and factors

- A multiple of a number is the product obtained when multiplying that number and an integer. The lowest common multiple (LCM) of two or more numbers is the lowest number that is a multiple of both (or all) of the numbers.
- A factor of a number is any number that will divide into the number exactly.
- The highest common factor (HCF) of two or more numbers is the highest number that is a factor of all the given numbers.

To find the LCM of a set of numbers, you can list the multiples of each number until you find the first multiple that is in the lists for all of the numbers in the set.

FAST FORWARD

You will use LCM again when you work with fractions to find the lowest common denominator of two or more fractions. See chapter 5. ▶

You need to work out whether to use LCM or HCF to find the answers. Problems involving LCM usually include repeating events. Problems involving HCF usually involve splitting things into smaller pieces or arranging things in equal groups or rows.

Read these problems carefully so that you will be able to recognise similar problems in future, even if you are not told to use HCF and LCM.

Exercise 1.2 A

1   Find the LCM of the given numbers.

a 9 and 18	b 12 and 18	c 15 and 18	d 24 and 12
e 36 and 9	f 4, 12, and 8	g 3, 9 and 24	h 12, 16 and 32

2   Find the HCF of the given numbers.

a 12 and 18	b 18 and 36	c 27 and 90	d 12 and 15
e 20 and 30	f 19 and 45	g 60 and 72	h 250 and 900

Exercise 1.2 B

1   Amira has two rolls of cotton fabric. One roll has 72 metres on it and the other has 90 metres on it. She wants to cut the fabric to make as many equal length pieces as possible of the longest possible length. How long should each piece be?

2   In a shopping mall promotion every 30th shopper gets a $10 voucher and every 120th shopper gets a free meal. How many shoppers must enter the mall before one receives a voucher and a free meal?

3   Amanda has 40 pieces of fruit and 100 sweets to share amongst the students in her class. She is able to give each student an equal number of pieces of fruit and an equal number of sweets. What is the largest possible number of students in her class?

4   Sam has sheets of green and yellow plastic that he wants to use to make a square chequerboard pattern on a coffee table top. Each sheet measures 210 cm by 154 cm. The squares are to be the maximum size possible. What will be the length of the side of each square and how many will he be able to cut from each sheet?

1.3   Prime numbers

- Prime numbers only have two factors: 1 and the number itself.
- Prime factors are factors of a number that are also prime numbers.
- You can write any number as a product of prime factors. But remember the number 1 itself is *not* a prime number so you cannot use it to write a number as the product of its prime factors.
- You can use the product of prime factors to find the HCF or LCM of two or more numbers.

You can use a tree diagram or division to find the prime factors of a composite whole number.

Exercise 1.3

1 Identify the prime numbers in each set.

    a 1, 2, 3, 4, 5, 6, 7, 8, 9, 10

    b 50, 51, 52, 53, 54, 55, 56, 57, 58, 59, 60

    c 95, 96, 97, 98, 99, 100, 101, 102, 103, 104, 105

2 Express the following numbers as a product of their prime factors.

a 36	**b** 65	**c** 64	**d** 84
e 80	**f** 1000	**g** 1270	**h** 1963

3 Find the LCM and the HCF of the following numbers by means of prime factors.

a 27 and 14	**b** 85 and 15	**c** 96 and 27	**d** 53 and 16
e 674 and 72	**f** 234 and 66	**g** 550 and 128	**h** 315 and 275

1.4 Powers and roots

- A number is squared (n^2) when it is multiplied by itself ($n \times n$).
- The square root ($\sqrt{n}$) of a number is the number that is multiplied by itself to get the number.
- A number is cubed (n^3) when it is multiplied by itself and then multiplied by itself again ($n \times n \times n$).
- The cube root ($\sqrt[3]{n}$) of a number is the number that is multiplied by itself twice to get the number.
- A number can be raised to any power (n^x). The value of x tells you how many times to multiply the number by itself.
- The $\sqrt[x]{}$ of a number is the number that was multiplied by itself x times to reach that number.

Exercise 1.4

1 Calculate.

a 3^2	**b** 18^2	**c** 21^2	**d** 25^2
e 6^3	**f** 15^3	**g** 18^3	**h** 35^3

2 Find these roots.

If you don't have a calculator, you can use the product of prime factors to find the square root or cube root of a number.

a $\sqrt{121}$	**b** $\sqrt[3]{512}$	**c** $\sqrt{441}$
d $\sqrt[3]{1331}$	**e** $\sqrt[3]{46656}$	**f** $\sqrt{2601}$
g $\sqrt{3136}$	**h** $\sqrt{729}$	**i** $\sqrt[4]{1296}$

3 Find all the square and cube numbers between 100 and 300.

4 Which of the following are square numbers and which are cube numbers?

1, 24, 49, 64, 256, 676, 625, 128

5 Simplify.

a $\sqrt{9}+\sqrt{16}$	**b** $\sqrt{9+16}$	**c** $\sqrt{64}+\sqrt{36}$
d $\sqrt{64+36}$	**e** $\sqrt{\dfrac{36}{4}}$	**f** $\left(\sqrt{25}\right)^2$

g $\dfrac{\sqrt{9}}{\sqrt{16}}$ **h** $\sqrt{169-144}$ **i** $\sqrt[3]{27}-\sqrt[3]{1}$

j $\sqrt{100\div 4}$ **k** $\sqrt{1}+\sqrt{\dfrac{9}{16}}$ **l** $\sqrt{16}\times\sqrt[3]{27}$

6 Evaluate.

a 4^3	**b** 7^4	**c** 16^4
d 12^3	**e** 20^3	**f** 10^5
g 13^3-3^5	**h** 3^3+2^7	**i** $\sqrt[3]{64}+4^5$
j $\left(2^4\right)^3$		

1.5 Working with directed numbers

- Integers are directed whole numbers.
- Negative integers are written with a minus (−) sign. Positive integers may be written with a plus (+) sign, but usually they are not.
- In real life, negative numbers are used to represent temperatures below zero; movements downwards or left; depths; distances below sea level; bank withdrawals and overdrawn amounts, and many more things.

Draw a number line to help you.

Exercise 1.5

1 If the temperature is 4 °C in the evening and it drops 7 °C overnight, what will the temperature be in the morning?

2 Which is colder in each pair of temperatures?

     a 0 °C or −2 °C   **b** 9 °C or −9 °C   **c** −4 °C or −12 °C

3 An office block has three basement levels (level −1, −2 and −3), a ground floor and 15 floors above the ground floor (1 to 15). Where will the lift be in the following situations?

     a Starts on ground and goes down one floor then up five?

     b Starts on level −3 and goes up 10 floors?

     c Starts on floor 12 and goes down 13 floors?

     d Starts on floor 15 and goes down 17 floors?

     e Starts on level −2, goes up seven floors and then down eight?

1.6 Order of operations

- When there is more than one operation to be done in a calculation you must work out the parts in brackets first. Then do any division or multiplication (from left to right) before adding and subtracting (from left to right).
- The word 'of' means × and a fraction line means divide.
- Long fraction lines and square or cube root signs act like brackets, indicating parts of the calculation that have to be done first.

Remember the order of operations using BODMAS:

Brackets
Of
Divide
Multiply
Add
Subtract

FAST FORWARD
The next section will remind you of the rules for rounding numbers. ▶

Exercise 1.6

1 Calculate and give your answer correct to two decimal places.

a $8 + 3 \times 6$

b $(8 + 3) \times 6$

c $8 \times 3 - 4 \div 5$

d $12.64 + 2.32 \times 1.3$

e $6.5 \times 1.3 - 5.06$

f $(6.7 \div 8) + 1.6$

g $1.453 + \dfrac{7.6}{3.2}$

h $\dfrac{5.34 + 3.315}{4.03}$

i $\dfrac{6.54}{2.3} - 1.08$

j $\dfrac{5.27}{1.4 \times 1.35}$

k $\dfrac{11.5}{2.9 - 1.43}$

l $\dfrac{0.23 \times 4.26}{1.32 + 3.43}$

m $8.9 - \dfrac{8.9}{10.4}$

n $\dfrac{12.6}{8.3} - \dfrac{1.98}{4.62}$

o $12.9 - 2.03^2$

p $(9.4 - 2.67)^3$

q $12.02^2 - 7.05^2$

r $\left(\dfrac{16.8}{9.3} - 1.01\right)^2$

s $\dfrac{4.07^2}{8.2 - 4.09}$

t $6.8 + \dfrac{1.4}{6.9} - \dfrac{1.2}{9.3}$

u $4.3 + \left(1.2 + \dfrac{1.6}{5}\right)^2$

v $\dfrac{6.1}{2.8} + \left(\dfrac{2.1}{1.6}\right)^2$

w $6.4 - (1.2^2 + 1.9^2)^2$

x $\left(4.8 - \dfrac{1}{9.6}\right) \times 4.3$

1.7 Rounding numbers

- You may be asked to round numbers to a given number of decimal places or to a given number of significant figures.
- To round to a decimal place:
  - look at the value of the digit to the right of the place you are rounding to
  - if this value is $\geqslant 5$ then you round up (add 1 to the digit you are rounding to)
  - if this value is $\leqslant 4$ then leave the digit you are rounding to as it is.
- To round to a significant figure:
  - the first non-zero digit (before or after the decimal place in a number) is the first significant figure
  - find the correct digit and then round off from that digit using the rules above.

Exercise 1.7

FAST FORWARD
Rounding is very useful when you have to estimate an answer. You will deal with this in more detail in chapter 5. ▶

1 Round these numbers to:

 i two decimal places
 ii one decimal place
 iii the nearest whole number.

a 5.6543

b 9.8774

c 12.8706

d 0.0098

e 10.099

f 45.439

g 13.999

h 26.001

Tip

If you are told what degree of accuracy to use, it is important to round to that degree. If you are not told, you can round to 3 significant figures.

2 Round each of these numbers to three significant figures.

a 53 217

b 712 984

c 17.364

d 0.007279

3 Round the following numbers to two significant figures.

a 35.8

b 5.234

c 12 345

d 0.00875

e 432 128

f 120.09

g 0.00456

h 10.002

Mixed exercise

Tip

Most modern scientific calculators apply the rules for order of operations automatically. But if there are brackets, fractions or roots in your calculation you need to enter these correctly on the calculator. When there is more than one term in the denominator, the calculator will divide by the first term only unless you enter brackets.

1 List the integers in the following set of numbers.

$\frac{3}{4}$ 24   0.65   −12 $3\frac{1}{2}$ 0   −15   0.66   −17

2 List the first five multiples of 15.

3 Find the lowest common multiple of 12 and 15.

4 Write each number as a product of its prime factors.

  a 196   **b** 1845   **c** 8820

5 Find the HCF of 28 and 42.

6 Simplify:

  a $\sqrt{100} \div \sqrt{4}$ **b** $\sqrt{100 \div 4}$ **c** $\left(\sqrt[3]{64}\right)^3$ **d** $4^3 + 9^2$

  e $23 \times \sqrt[4]{1296}$ **f** $-24 \times \sqrt[3]{343}$ **g** $\left(\frac{1}{2}\right)^{-2} + \sqrt[5]{1}$ **h** $\left(\frac{1}{2}\right)^{-4} - \sqrt[6]{46\,656}$

7 Calculate. Give your answer correct to two decimal places.

  a $\frac{5.4 \times 12.2}{4.1}$ **b** $\frac{12.2^2}{3.9^2}$ **c** $\frac{12.65}{2.04} + 1.7 \times 4.3$

  d $\frac{3.8 \times 12.6}{4.35}$ **e** $\frac{2.8 \times 4.2^2}{3.3^2 \times 6.2^2}$ **f** $2.5 - \left(3.1 + \frac{0.5}{5}\right)^2 (3.3)^2$

8 Round each number to three significant figures.

  a 1235.6   **b** 0.76513   **c** 0.0237548   **d** 31.4596

9 Naresh has 6 400 square tiles. Is it possible for him to arrange these to make a perfect square? Justify your answer.

10 Ziggy has a square sheet of fabric with sides 120 cm long. Is this big enough to cover a square table of area 1.4 m²? Explain your answer.

11 A cube has a volume of 3.375 m³. How high is it?

Making sense of algebra

2.1 Using letters to represent unknown values

- Letters in algebra are called variables because they can have many different values (the value varies). Any letter can be used as a variable, but x and y are used most often.
- A number on its own is called a constant.
- A term is a group of numbers and/or variables combined by the operations multiplying and/or dividing only.
- An algebraic expression links terms by using the + and − operation signs. An expression does not have an equals sign (unlike an equation). An expression could have just one term.

Exercise 2.1

> **Tip**
> An expression in terms of x means that the variable letter used in the expression is x.

1 Write expressions, in terms of x, to represent:

   a a number times seven

   b the sum of a number and twelve

   c five times a number minus two

   d the difference between a third of a number and twice the number.

2 A boy is p years old.

   a How old will the boy be in five years' time?

   b How old was the boy four years ago?

   c His father is four times the boy's age. How old is the father?

> Being able to translate a word problem into an expression is a useful strategy for problem solving. Remember you can use any letter as a variable as long as you say what it means.

3 Three people win a prize of $\$x$.

   a If they share the prize equally, how much will each of them receive?

   b If the prize is divided so that the first person gets half as much money as the second person and the third person gets three times as much as the second person, how much will each receive?

2.2 Substitution

- Substitution involves replacing variables with given numbers to work out the value of an expression. For example, you may be told to evaluate $5x$ when $x = -2$. To do this you work out $5 \times (-2) = -10$

Exercise 2.2

REWIND

Remember that the BODMAS rules always apply in these calculations. ◄

1 Evaluate the following expressions if $x = 5$.

 a $4x$ **b** $12x$ **c** $3x - 4$ **d** x^2

 e $-2x^2$ **f** $14 - x$ **g** $x^3 - 10x$ **h** $x^3 - x^2$

 i $3(x - 2)$ **j** $\dfrac{6x}{2}$ **k** $\dfrac{4x}{10}$ **l** $\dfrac{80}{x}$

 m $\dfrac{12x}{4}$ **n** $\dfrac{2x - 4}{2}$ **o** $\sqrt{9x^2}$ **p** $\dfrac{3x^3}{2x^2}$

Take special care when substituting negative numbers. If you replace x with −3 in the expression $4x$, you will obtain $4 \times -3 = -12$, but in the expression $-4x$, you will obtain $-4 \times -3 = 12$.

2 Given that $a = 2$, $b = 5$ and $c = -1$, evaluate:

 a abc **b** $2bc$ **c** $\dfrac{b^2 + c}{a}$ **d** $4ac - 3b$

 e $6c - 2ab$ **f** $2(ab - 4c)$ **g** $(abc)^3$ **h** $2(a^2b)^3$

3 The formula for finding the area (A) of a triangle is $A = \dfrac{1}{2}bh$, where b is the length of the base and h is the perpendicular height of the triangle.

 Find the area of a triangle if:

 a the base is 12 cm and the height is 9 cm

 b the base is 2.5 m and the height is 1.5 m

 c the base is 21 cm and the height is half as long as the base

 d the height is 2 cm and the base is the cube of the height.

2.3 Simplifying expressions

- To simplify an expression you add or subtract like terms.
- Like terms are those that have exactly the same variables (including powers of variables).
- You can also multiply and divide to simplify expressions. Both like and unlike terms can be multiplied or divided.

Exercise 2.3

Remember, like terms must have exactly the same variables with exactly the same indices. So $3x$ and $2x$ are like terms but $3x^2$ and $2x$ are not like terms.

1 Simplify the following expressions.

 a $5m + 6n - 3m$ **b** $5x + 4 + x - 2$ **c** $a^2 + 4a + 2a - 5$ **d** $y^2 - 4y - y - 2$

 e $3x^2 + 6x - 8x + 3$ **f** $x^2y + 3x^2y - 2yx$ **g** $2ab - 4ac + 3ba$

 h $x^2 + 2x - 4 + 3x^2 - y + 3x - 1$

2 Simplify.

a $4x \times 3y$ **b** $4a \times 2b$ **c** $x \times x$ **d** $3 \times -2x$

e $-6m \times 5n$ **f** $3xy \times 2x$ **g** $-2xy \times -3y^2$ **h** $-2xy \times 2x^2$

i $12ab \div 3a$ **j** $12x \div 48xy$ **k** $\dfrac{33abc}{11ca}$ **l** $\dfrac{45mn}{20n}$

m $\dfrac{80xy^2}{12x^2y}$ **n** $\dfrac{-36x^3}{-12xy}$ **o** $\dfrac{y}{x} \times \dfrac{2y}{x}$ **p** $\dfrac{xy}{2} \times \dfrac{y}{x}$

q $5a \times \dfrac{3a}{4}$ **r** $7 \times \dfrac{-2y}{5}$ **s** $\dfrac{x}{4} \times \dfrac{2}{3y}$ **t** $\dfrac{3x}{5} \times \dfrac{9x}{2}$

2.4 Working with brackets

- You can remove brackets from an expression by multiplying everything inside the brackets by the value (or values) in front of the bracket.
- Removing brackets is also called expanding the expression.
- When you remove brackets in part of an expression you may end up with like terms. Add or subtract any like terms to simplify the expression fully.
- In general terms $a(b + c) = ab + ac$

Exercise 2.4

1 Expand.

a $3(x+2)$ **b** $2(x-4)$ **c** $-2(x+3)$ **d** $-3(3-2x)$

e $x(x+3)$ **f** $x(2-x)$ **g** $-x(2+2x)$ **h** $3x(x-3)$

i $-2x(2-5x)$ **j** $-(x-2)$ **k** $-2x(2y-2x)$ **l** $-x(2x-4)$

2 Remove the brackets and simplify where possible.

a $2x(x-2)$ **b** $(y-3)x$ **c** $(x-2)-3x$ **d** $-2x-(x-2)$

e $(x-3)(-2x)$ **f** $2(x+1)-(1-x)$ **g** $x(x^2-2x-1)$

h $-x(1-x)+2(x+3)-4$

3 Remove the brackets and simplify where possible.

a $2x(\frac{1}{2}x+\frac{1}{4})$ **b** $-3x(x-y)-2x(y-2x)$

c $-2(4x^2-2x-1)x$ **d** $(x+y)-(\frac{1}{2}x-\frac{1}{2}y)$

e $2x(2x-2)-x(x+2)$ **f** $x(1-x)+x(2x-5)-2x(1+3x)$

2.5 Indices

- An index (also called a power or exponent) shows how many times the base is multiplied by itself.
- x^2 means $x \times x$ and $(3y)^4$ means $3y \times 3y \times 3y \times 3y$.
- The laws of indices are used to simplify algebraic terms and expressions. Make sure you know the laws and understand how they work (see below).
- When an expression contains negative indices you apply the same laws as for other indices to simplify it.

Tip
Memorise this summary of the **index laws**:

1. $x^m \times x^n = x^{m+n}$ (1)
2. $x^m \div x^n = x^{m-n}$ (2)
3. $(x^m)^n = x^{mn}$ (3)
4. $x^0 = 1$ (4)
5. $x^{-m} = \dfrac{1}{x^m}$ (5)
6. $x^{\frac{m}{n}} = \left(x^{\frac{1}{n}}\right)^m = \left(\sqrt[n]{x}\right)^m$

Remember, a fraction is the top value divided by the bottom value. This means $\dfrac{x^m}{x^n}$ is the same as $x^m \div x^n$ so you can use the second index law to simplify it.

Tip
Apply the index laws and work in this order:

- simplify any terms in brackets
- apply the multiplication law (1 above) to numerators and then to denominators
- cancel numbers if you can
- apply the division law (2 above) if the same letter appears in the numerator and denominator
- express your answer using positive indices

Exercise 2.5 A

1 Simplify.

a $x^9 \times x^2$ b $y^{10} \times y^3$ c $2x \times 3x^2$ d $-2x^2 \times -3x^6$

e $x^2 y^3 \times x^3 y$ f $-2x \times 8x \times -3x^2$ g $(2x^2 y)(xy)$ h $-3x^4 \times 9x^8$

2 Simplify.

a $2x^5 \div 3x^3$ b $18x^3 yz^2 \div 6xyz^2$ c $12xy^3 \div 18xy^2$ d $-6x \div -12x^2$

e $21x^2 y \div 14x^4 y^6$ f $\dfrac{12x^3 yz^2}{6xy^4 z}$ g $\dfrac{14x^2}{2x^3}$ h $\dfrac{16x^2 y}{4xy^2}$

i $\dfrac{x^2 y}{3xy^2}$ j $\dfrac{x^7 y^3}{x^4 y^5}$ k $\dfrac{36x^2 yz^4}{-24xyz}$ l $\dfrac{9x^3 y^{-2}}{18x^{-2} y^4}$

3 Rewrite each of the following using positive indices only.

a 3^{-2} b $3x^{-3}$ c $\dfrac{xy^{-1}}{2}$

d $(xy)^{-1}$ e $(8xy)^{-2}$ f $\dfrac{1}{(4xy)^{-2}}$

g $y^{-5} \times y^6$ h $x^3 y^{-1} \times y^{-3}$ i $x^3 y \times x^{-1} y^{-3}$

j $y^6 (x^3)^{-4} \times (x^3 y^{-2})^2$ k $(3xy^3)^{-2} \times (2x^3 y)^3$ l $\dfrac{4y^{-2}}{7x^{-3}}$

4 Simplify.

a $(x^3)^2$ b $(-2x^3)^3$ c $\left(\dfrac{2x^2}{x}\right)^4$ d $(x^9)^3$

e $(-xy^2)^9$ f $(x^3 y^2)^4$ g $-2(xy)^3$ h $2x^2(2x)^3$

i $\dfrac{(xy^2)^3}{x^3 y^6}$ j $(xy)^4 (x^4)^3$ k $(3x^y)^y$ l $-(2x^2)^3$

Exercise 2.5 B

1 Simplify.

a $\dfrac{x^4 y \times y^2 x^6}{x^4 y^5}$ b $\dfrac{2x^2 y^4 \times 3x^3 y}{2xy^4}$ c $\dfrac{2x^5 y^4 \times 2xy^3}{2x^2 y^5 \times 3x^2 y^3}$

d $\dfrac{x^3 y^7}{xy^4} \times \dfrac{x^2 y^8}{x^3 y}$ e $\dfrac{2x^7 y^2}{4x^3 y^7} \times \dfrac{10x^8 y^4}{2x^3 y^2}$ f $\dfrac{x^9 y^6}{x^4 y^2} \div \dfrac{x^3 y^2}{x^5 y}$

2 Making sense of algebra

Tip

You can use simplified expressions with negative indices, such as $5x^{-4}$.
If, however, the question states positive indices only, you can use the law $x^{-m} = \dfrac{1}{x^m}$ so that $5x^{-4} = \dfrac{5}{x^4}$.
Similarly, $\dfrac{y}{x^{-2}} = x^2 y$.

g $\dfrac{10x^5 y^2}{9x^6 y^6} \div \dfrac{3x^3 y}{5x^7 y^4}$
h $\dfrac{7y^3 x^2}{5y^5 x^4} \div \dfrac{5x^6 y^2}{7x^5 y^3}$
i $\dfrac{\left(x^5 y\right)^2 \times \left(x^3 y^4\right)^2}{\left(x^3 y^3\right)^3}$

j $\dfrac{\left(2x^4 y^2\right)^3}{\left(y^3 x^2\right)^3} \times \dfrac{\left(x^4 y^4\right)^2}{3\left(x^2 y\right)^2}$
k $\left(\dfrac{x^2}{y^4}\right)^3 \times \left(\dfrac{x^5}{y^2}\right)^2$
l $\dfrac{\left(5x^3 y^2\right)^3}{4x^7 y^6} \div \left(\dfrac{2xy^3}{5x^2 y^4}\right)^2$

2 Simplify each expression and give your answer using positive indices only.

a $\dfrac{x^5 y^{-4}}{x^{-3} y^{-2}}$
b $\dfrac{x^{-4} y^3}{x^2 y^{-1}} \times \dfrac{x^7 y^{-5}}{x^{-4} y^3}$
c $\dfrac{\left(2x^{-3} y^{-1}\right)^3}{\left(y^2 x^{-2}\right)^2}$

d $\left(\dfrac{x}{y^3}\right)^{-1} \div \dfrac{\left(x^2\right)^4}{y^{-3}}$
e $\dfrac{x^{-10}}{\left(y^{-4}\right)^2} \div \left(\dfrac{y^2}{x^3}\right)^{-4}$
f $\left(\dfrac{x^4 y^{-1}}{x^5 y^{-3}}\right)^2 \times \dfrac{\left(x^{-2} y^6\right)^2}{2\left(xy^3\right)^{-2}}$

3 Simplify.

a $x^{\frac{1}{4}} \times x^{\frac{1}{4}}$
b $x^{\frac{1}{3}} \times x^{\frac{1}{5}}$
c $\dfrac{x^{\frac{1}{2}}}{x^{\frac{1}{3}}}$
d $\left(x^{\frac{1}{3}}\right)^{\frac{1}{3}}$

e $\left(64x^6\right)^{\frac{1}{2}}$
f $\left(8x^9 y\right)^{\frac{1}{3}}$
g $\sqrt{xy^8}$
h $\left(\dfrac{x^6}{y^2}\right)^{\frac{1}{2}}$

i $\left(x^{\frac{1}{2}}\right)^8 \times \dfrac{x^2}{x^3}$
j $\left(x^6 y^3\right)^{\frac{1}{3}} \times \left(x^{-8} y^{-10}\right)^{\frac{1}{2}}$
k $\left(xy^3\right)^{\frac{1}{2}} \times \dfrac{x^{\frac{1}{2}} y^{\frac{1}{2}}}{xy^4}$

Mixed exercise

1 Write each of the following as an algebraic expression. Use x to represent 'the number'.

a A number increased by 12.
b A number decreased by four.
c Five times a number.
d A number divided by three.
e The product of a number and four.
f A quarter of a number.
g A number subtracted from 12.
h The difference between a number and its cube.

2 Determine the value of $x^2 - 5x$ if:

a $x = 2$
b $x = -3$
c $x = \dfrac{1}{3}$

3 Evaluate each expression if $a = -1$, $b = 2$ and $c = 0$.

a $\dfrac{-2a + 3b}{2ab}$
b $\dfrac{b(c - a)}{b - a}$
c $\dfrac{a - b^2}{c - a^2}$

d $\dfrac{3 - 2(a - 1)}{c - a(b - 1)}$
e $a^3 b^2 - 2a^2 + a^4 b^2 - ac^3$

4 **a** $M = 9ab$. Find M when $a = 7$ and $b = 10$.
b $V - rs = 2uw$. Find V when $r = 8$, $s = 4$, $u = 6$ and $w = 1$.
c $\dfrac{V}{30} = \sqrt{h}$. Find V when $h = 25$.
d $P - y = x^2$. Find P when $x = 2$ and $y = 8$.

Unit 1: Algebra   11

5 Remove the brackets and simplify as fully as possible.

a $2(y+5)$ b $4(y-1)$ c $3(2x+5)$ d $4(3x-2y)$

e $x(y+2)$ f $2(10x-7y+3z)$ g $2x(3x+1)$ h $2(x+3)+1$

i $6(x+3)-2x$ j $3x+2(6x-3y)$

6 Simplify each of the following expressions as fully as possible.

a $3a+4b+6a-3b$ b $x^2+4x-x-2$ c $-2a^2b(2a^2-3b^2)$

d $2x(x-3)-(x-4)-2x^2$ e $16x^2y \div 4y^2x$ f $\dfrac{10x^2-5xy}{2x}$

7 Expand and simplify if possible.

a $2(4x-3)+3(x+1)$ b $3x(2x+3)-2(4-3x)$

c $x(x+2)+3x-3(x^2-4)$ d $x^2(x+3)-2x^3-(x-5)$

8 Simplify. Give all answers with positive indices only.

a $\dfrac{15x^7}{18x^2}$ b $5x^2 \times \dfrac{3x^5}{x^7}$ c $\dfrac{\left(x^3\right)^4}{\left(x^2\right)^8}$

d $\left(2xy^2\right)^4$ e $\left(\dfrac{4x^3}{y^5}\right)^3$ f $\left(x^3y\right)^2 \times \dfrac{\left(x^2y^4\right)^3}{\left(xy^2\right)^3}$

g $\left(2xy^3\right)^{-2} \times \left(3x^2y\right)^3$ h $\dfrac{\left(x^{-3}y^2\right)^4}{2\left(xy^2\right)^{-3}} \div \left(\dfrac{x^{-3}y^3}{x^2y^{-1}}\right)^2$

9 Evaluate.

a $4^{\frac{1}{2}}$ b $-(10\,000)^{\frac{1}{4}}$ c $16^{\frac{1}{4}}$ d $\left(\dfrac{8}{27}\right)^{-\frac{1}{3}}$

3 Lines, angles and shapes

3.1 Lines and angles

- Angles can be classified according to their size:
  - acute angles are $< 90°$
  - right angles are $90°$
  - obtuse angles are $> 90°$ but $< 180°$
  - reflex angles are $> 180°$ but $< 360°$.
- Two angles that add up to $90°$ are called complementary angles. Two angles that add up to $180°$ are called supplementary angles.
- The sum of adjacent angles on a straight line is $180°$.
- The sum of the angles around a point is $360°$.
- When two lines intersect (cross), two pairs of vertically opposite angles are formed. Vertically opposite angles are equal.
- When two parallel lines are cut by a transversal, alternate angles are equal, corresponding angles are equal and co-interior angles add up to $180°$.
- When alternate or corresponding angles are equal, or when co-interior angles add up to $180°$, the lines are parallel.

Exercise 3.1 A

1 Estimate the size of each angle and say what type of angle it is. Then measure each angle with a protractor and give its size in degrees.

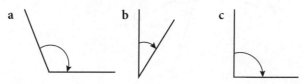

Draw a diagram to model problems and make it easier to find the solution.

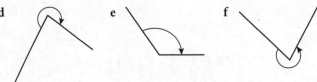

d   **e**   **f**

2 Look at the clock face on the left. Calculate the following.

a The angle between the hands of the clock at:

    i 3 a.m.   **ii** 1800 hours.

b Through how many degrees does the hour hand move between 4 p.m. and 5 p.m.?

c Through how many degrees does the minute hand turn in one hour?

d A clock shows 12 noon. What will the time be when the minute hand has moved 270° clockwise?

3 Will doubling an acute angle always produce an obtuse angle? Explain your answer.

4 Will halving an obtuse angle always produce an acute angle? Explain your answer.

5 What is the complement of each the following angles?

    a 45°   **b** 62°   **c** $x°$ **d** $(90 - x)°$

6 What is the supplement of each of the following angles?

    a 45°   **b** 90°   **c** 104°   **d** $x°$

    e $(180 - x)°$ **f** $(90 - x)°$ **g** $(90 + x)°$ **h** $(2x - 40)$

! Tip
You need to be able to use the relationships between lines and angles to calculate the values of unknown angles.

Exercise 3.1 B

In this exercise, calculate (do not measure from the diagrams) the values of the lettered angles. You should also state your reasons.

1 In the following diagram, *PQ* and *RS* are straight lines. Calculate the sizes of angles *x*, *y* and *z*.

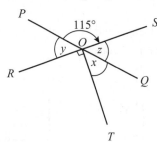

2 In the following diagram, *MN* and *PQ* are straight lines. Find the size of angle *a*.

Remember, give reasons for statements. Use these abbreviations:

Comp angles

Supp angles

Angles on line

Angles round point

VO angles

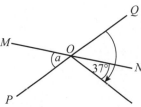

angle *QOR* = 85°

3 Calculate the value of *x* in each of the following figures.

a

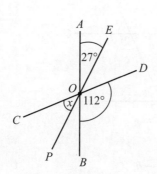

b

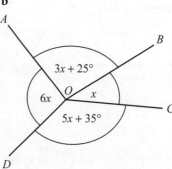

Exercise 3.1 C

1 In this figure the size of angle *AGH* is given. Calculate the size of all the other angles giving reasons.

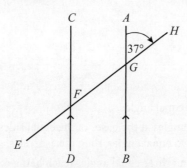

2 Find the values of the angles marked with the letters *x*, *y* and *z* in each diagram. Give reasons for any statements you make.

a

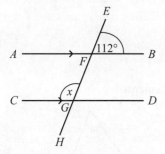

b

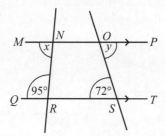

c

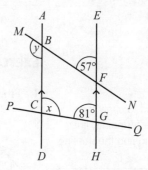

d

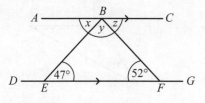

e

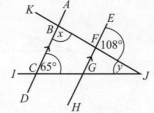

f

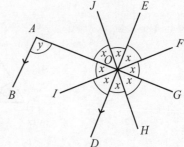

3 Calculate the value of x and y in each of the following figures. Give reasons for your answers.

a

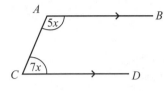

b

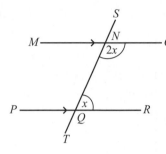

c

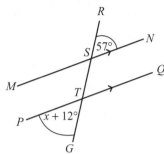

d

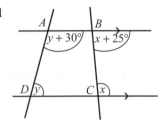

e

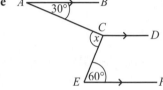

f

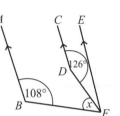

3.2 Triangles

- Scalene triangles have no equal sides and no equal angles.
- Isosceles triangles have two equal sides. The angles at the bases of the equal sides are equal in size. The converse is also true – if a triangle has two equal angles, then it is isosceles.
- Equilateral triangles have three equal sides and three equal angles (each being 60°).
- The sum of the interior angles of any triangle is 180°.
- The exterior angle of a triangle is equal to the sum of the two opposite interior angles.

Exercise 3.2

REWIND

You may also need to apply the angle relationships for points, lines and parallel lines to find the missing angles in triangles. ◀

1 Find the angles marked with letters. Give reasons for any statements.

a

b

c

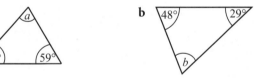

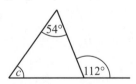

d

e

f

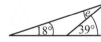

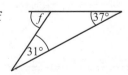

g

h

i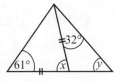

j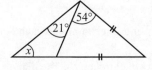

k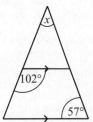

l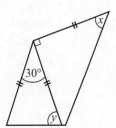

2 Calculate the value of *x* and hence find the size of the marked angles.

a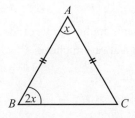

b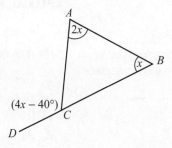

c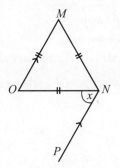

d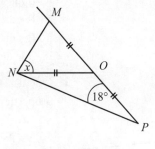

e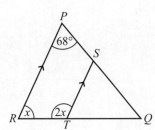

f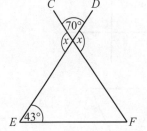

3.3 Quadrilaterals

- A quadrilateral is a four-sided shape.
  - A trapezium has one pair of parallel sides.
  - A kite has two pairs of adjacent sides equal in length. The diagonals intersect at 90° and the longer diagonal bisects the shorter one. Only one pair of opposite angles is equal. The diagonals bisect the opposite angles.
  - A parallelogram has opposite sides equal and parallel. The opposite angles are equal in size and the diagonals bisect each other.
  - A rectangle has opposite sides equal and parallel and interior angles each equal to 90°. The diagonals are equal in length and they bisect each other.
  - A rhombus is a parallelogram with all four sides equal in length. The diagonals bisect each other at 90° and bisect the opposite angles.
  - A square has four equal sides and four angles each equal to 90°. The opposite sides are parallel. The diagonals are equal in length, they bisect each other at right angles and they bisect the opposite angles.
- The sum of the interior angles of a quadrilateral is 360°.

Exercise 3.3

> **REWIND**
>
> The angle relationships for parallel lines will apply when a quadrilateral has parallel sides. ◀

1 Each of the following statements applies to one or more quadrilaterals. For each one, name the quadrilateral(s) to which it always applies.

- **a** All sides are equal in length
- **b** All angles are equal in size
- **c** The diagonals are the same length
- **d** The diagonals bisect each other
- **e** The angles are all 90° and the diagonals bisect each other
- **f** Opposite angles are equal in size
- **g** The diagonals intersect at right angles
- **h** The diagonals bisect the opposite angles
- **i** One diagonal divides the quadrilateral into two isosceles triangles.

2 Calculate the size of the marked angles in the following figures. Give reasons or state the properties you are using.

a
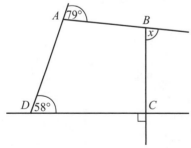

b
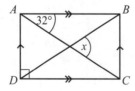

c
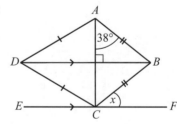

d
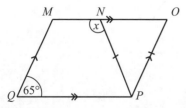

e

f
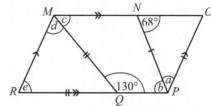

3.4 Polygons

- A polygon is a two-dimensional shape with three or more sides. Polygons are named according the number of sides they have:

  - triangle (3)   - heptagon (7)
  - quadrilateral (4)   - octagon (8)
  - pentagon (5)   - nonagon (9)
  - hexagon (6)   - decagon (10).

- A regular polygon has all its sides equal and all its angles equal.
- The interior angle sum of any polygon can be worked out using the formula $(n - 2) \times 180°$ where n is the number of sides. Once you have the angle sum, you can find the size of one angle of a regular polygon by dividing the total by the number of angles.
- The sum of the exterior angles of any convex polygon is $360°$.

Exercise 3.4

> **Tip**
>
> If you can't remember the formula, you can find the size of one interior angle of a regular polygon using the fact that the exterior angles add up to $360°$. Divide 360 by the number of angles to find the size of one exterior angle. Then use the fact that the exterior and interior angles form a straight line ($180°$) to work out the size of the interior angle.

1 For a regular hexagon.

   a Calculate the size on one exterior angle.
   b Find the sum of the interior angles.
   c What is the size of each interior angle?

2 Find the sum of the interior angles of:

   a a regular octagon
   b a regular decagon
   c a regular 15-sided polygon.

3 A coin is made in the shape of a regular 7-sided polygon. Calculate the size of each interior angle.

4 The interior angle of a regular polygon is $162°$. How many sides does the polygon have?

5 One exterior angle of a regular polygon is $14.4°$.

   a What is the size of each interior angle?
   b How many sides does the polygon have?

3.5 Circles

- A circle is a set of points equidistant from a fixed centre. Half a circle is a semi-circle.
- The perimeter of a circle is called its circumference.
- The distance across a circle (through the centre) is called its diameter. A radius is half a diameter.
- An arc is part of the circumference of a circle.
- A chord is a line joining two points on the circumference. A chord cuts the circle into two segments.
- A 'slice' of a circle, made by two radii and the arc between them on the circumference, is called a sector.
- A tangent is a line that touches a circle at only one point.

Exercise 3.5

Copy and complete the table below, naming each part of the circle and giving its definition.

Diagram	Name	Definition

Diagram	Name	Definition

3.6 Construction

- You need to be able to use a ruler and a pair of compasses to construct triangles (given the lengths of three sides).

Tip

Always start with a rough sketch. Label your rough sketch so you know what lengths you need to measure.

Exercise 3.6

1 These steps for constructing a triangle of sides 9 cm, 7 cm and 15 cm using only a ruler and a pair of compasses have been mixed up.

   a Write the letters A to E in a correct order.
   b Why is there more than one way of ordering them?
   A   At the endpoint of the line segment draw an arc with a radius of 7 cm.
   B   Draw a line segment 15 cm long.
   C   Draw a line from the intersection to each endpoint.
   D   At the endpoint of the line segment, draw an arc with radius of 9 cm.
   E   Find the point where the two arcs intersect.

2 Construct triangle ABC with $AC = 7$ cm, $CB = 6$ cm and $AB = 8$ cm.

3 Construct triangle MNO with $MN = 4.5$ cm, $NO = 5.5$ cm and $MO = 8$ cm.

4 Construct triangle *DEF* with *DE* = 100 mm, *FE* = 70 mm and *DF* = 50 mm. What type of triangle is *DEF*?

5 Nino is trying to construct triangle *ABC* with sides *AB* = 7 cm, *BC* = 3 cm and *AC* = 8 cm. He started by drawing an 8 cm long line segment and then used a pair of compasses to draw arcs like this:

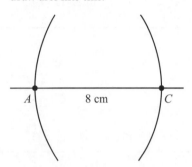

a What has he done incorrectly?

b Construct the triangle correctly.

Mixed exercise

1 Write a correct mathematical definition for each of the following:

  a alternate angles   **b** an isosceles triangle

  c a kite   **d** a rhombus

  e a regular polygon   **f** an octagon.

2 Find the value of the marked angles in each of the following.

a

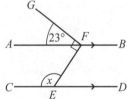

b

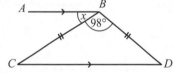

c

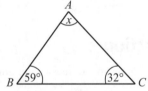

d

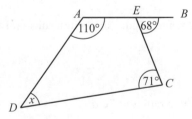

e

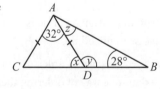

f

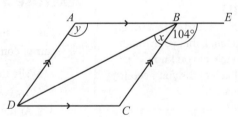

g

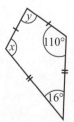

h

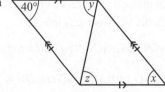

3 For each shape combination find the size of angle *x*. All shapes in both figures are regular polygons.

a

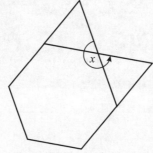

b

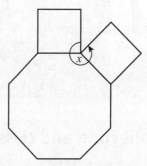

4 Use the diagram of the circle with centre *O* to answer these questions.

a What are the correct mathematical names for:

   i *DO*   **ii** *AB*   **iii** *AC*?

b Four radii are shown on the diagram. Name them.

c If *OB* is 12.4 cm long, how long is *AC*?

d Draw a copy of the circle and on to it draw the tangent to the circle that passes through point *B*.

5 Construct triangle *ABC* with *AB* = *BC* = *AC* = 6.5 cm.

6 Points *A* and *B* are the centres of two overlapping circles of diameter 9 cm.

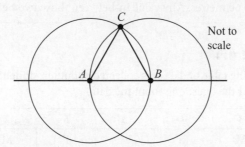

Not to scale

Accurately construct the triangle without drawing the circles.

4 Collecting, organising and displaying data

4.1 Collecting and classifying data

- Data is a set of facts, numbers or other information, collected to try to answer a question.
- Primary data is 'original' data and can be collected by measuring, observation, doing experiments, carrying out surveys or asking people to complete questionnaires.
- Secondary data is data drawn from a non-original source. For example you could find the area of each of the world's oceans by referring to an atlas.
- You can classify data as qualitative or quantitative.
- Qualitative data is non-numeric such as colour, make of vehicle or favourite flavour.
- Quantitative data is numerical data that was counted or measured. For example age, marks in a test, shoe size, height.
- Quantitative data can be discrete or continuous.
- Discrete data can only take certain values and is usually something counted. For example, the number of children in your family. There are no in-between values; you can't have $2\frac{1}{2}$ children in a family.
- Continuous data can take any value and is usually something measured. For example the heights of trees in a rainforest could range from 50 to 60 metres. Any value in-between those two heights is possible.

Exercise 4.1

The following table of data was collected about ten students in a high school. Study the table and then answer the questions about the data.

Student	1	2	3	4	5	6	7	8	9	10
Gender	F	F	M	M	M	F	M	F	F	M
Height (m)	1.55	1.61	1.63	1.60	1.61	1.62	1.64	1.69	1.61	1.65
Shoe size	3	4	7	6	9	7	8	7	5	10
Mass (kg)	40	51	52	54	60	43	55	56	51	55
Eye colour	Br	Gr	Gr	Br	Br	Br	Br	Gr	Bl	Br
Hair colour	Bl	Bl	Blo	Br	Br	Br	Bl	Bl	Bl	Bl
No. of brothers/ sisters	0	3	4	2	1	2	3	1	0	3

a Which of these data categories are qualitative?

b Which of these data categories are quantitative?

c Which sets of numerical data are discrete data?

d Which sets of numerical data are continuous data?

e How do you think each set of data was collected? Give a reason for your answers.

4.2 Organising data

- Once data has been collected, it needs to be arranged and organised so that it is easier to work with, interpret and make inferences about.
- Tally tables, frequency tables and stem-and-leaf diagrams are used to organise data and to show the totals of different values or categories. A back-to-back stem-and-leaf diagram can be used to show two sets of related data.
- When you have a large set of numerical data, with lots of different scores, you can group the data into intervals called class intervals. Class intervals should not overlap.
- A two way table can be used to show the frequency of results for two or more sets of data.

Exercise 4.2

In data handling, the word **frequency** means the number of times a score or observation occurs.

1 Here are the marks obtained by 40 students in an assignment. The assignment was out of 10.

6	5	6	7	4	5	8	6	7	10
7	6	5	6	1	9	4	4	2	6
5	5	7	3	4	5	8	3	5	8
10	9	9	7	5	5	7	6	4	2

Copy and complete this tally table to organise the data.

Mark	Tally	Frequency
1		
2		

2 Nika tossed a dice 40 times and got these results.

6	6	6	5	4	3	2	6	5	4
1	1	3	2	5	4	3	3	3	2
1	6	5	5	4	4	3	2	5	4
6	3	2	4	2	1	2	2	1	5

a Copy and complete this frequency table to organise the data.

Score	1	2	3	4	5	6
Frequency						

b Do the results suggest that this is a fair dice or not? Give a reason for your answer.

3 These are the percentage scores of 50 students in an examination.

54	26	60	40	55	82	67	59	57	70
67	44	63	56	46	48	55	63	42	58
45	54	76	65	63	61	49	54	54	53
67	56	69	57	38	57	51	55	59	78
65	52	55	78	69	71	73	88	80	91

Score	Frequency
0–29	
30–39	
40–49	
50–59	
60–69	
70–79	
80–100	

a Copy and complete this grouped frequency table to organise the results.

b How many students scored 70% or more?

c How many students scored lower than 40%?

d How many students scored 40% or more but less than 60%?

e The first and last class interval in the table are greater than the others. Suggest why this is the case.

f Draw an ordered stem-and-leaf diagram to show the data. What advantage does it have over the frequency table?

4 This is a section of the table you worked with in Exercise 4.1.

Student	1	2	3	4	5	6	7	8	9	10
Gender	F	F	M	M	M	F	M	F	F	M
Eye colour	Br	Gr	Gr	Br	Br	Br	Br	Gr	Bl	Br
Hair colour	Bl	Bl	Blo	Br	Br	Br	Bl	Bl	Bl	Bl
No. of siblings (brothers/sisters)	0	3	4	2	1	2	3	1	0	3

a Copy and complete this two way table using data from the table.

Eye colour	Brown	Blue	Green
Male			
Female			

b Draw up and complete two similar two way tables of your own to show the hair colour and number of brothers or sisters by gender.

c Write a sentence to summarise what you found out for each table.

5 A traffic department installed a camera and counted the number of cars passing an intersection every hour for 24 hours.

These are the results:

1	5	7	12	16	23	31	31
51	35	31	33	29	24	43	48
41	39	37	20	19	18	12	2

a Draw an ordered stem-and-leaf diagram to show the data.

b What is the maximum number of cars that passed through in an hour during this period?

4.3 Using charts to display data

- Charts usually help you to see patterns and trends in data more easily than in tables.
- Pictograms use symbols to show the frequency of data in different categories. They are useful for discrete, categorical and ungrouped data.
- Bar charts are useful for categorical and ungrouped data. A bar chart has bars of equal width which are equally spaced.
- Bar charts can be drawn as horizontal or vertical charts. They can also show two or more sets of data on the same set of axes.
- Pie charts are circular graphs that use sectors of circle to show the proportion of data in each category.
- All charts should have a heading and clearly labelled scales, axes or keys.

Exercise 4.3

Number of students in each year

Year 8	♀♀♀♀♀♀♀♀♀
Year 9	♀♀♀♀♀♀
Year 10	♀♀♀♀♀♀♀
Year 11	♀♀♀♀♀♀♀♀♀♀
Year 12	♀♀♀♀♀♀♀♀

Key

♀ = 30 students

1 Study the diagram carefully and answer the questions about it.

a What type of chart is this?

b What does the chart show?

c What does each full symbol represent?

d How are 15 students shown on the chart?

e How many students are there in year 8?

f Which year group has the most students? How many are there in this year group?

g Do you think these are accurate or rounded figures? Why?

2 Naresh did a survey to find out how much time his friends spent on social media during the day. These are his results.

Person	Alain	Li	Zayn	David
Time (hours)	$2\frac{1}{2}$	$1\frac{1}{3}$	$4\frac{3}{4}$	$2\frac{1}{4}$

Draw a pictogram to show this data.

3 Study the two bar charts below.

a What does chart A show?

b How many boys are there in Class 10A?

c How many students are there in 10A altogether?

d What does chart B show?

e Which sport is most popular with boys?

f Which sport is most popular with girls?

g How many students chose basketball as their favourite sport?

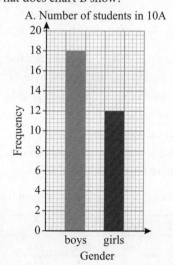

A. Number of students in 10A

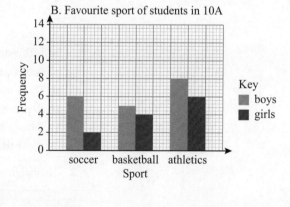

B. Favourite sport of students in 10A

Key
- boys
- girls

> **! Tip**
> Choose symbols that are easy to draw and to divide into parts. If it is not given, choose a suitable scale for your symbols so you don't have to draw too many.

> **! Tip**
> Compound bar charts show two or more sets of data on the same pair of axes. A key is needed to show which set each bar represents.

4 The table below shows the type of food that a group of students in a hostel chose for breakfast.

	Cereal	Hot porridge	Bread
Girls	8	16	12
Boys	2	12	10

a Draw a single bar chart to show the choice of cereal against bread.

b Draw a compound bar chart to show the breakfast food choice for girls and boys.

Tip

To work out the percentage that an angle in a pie chart represents, use the formula:

$$\frac{n}{360} \times 100$$

where n is the size of the angle.

5 Jyoti recorded the number and type of 180 vehicles passing her home in Bangalore. She drew this pie chart to show her results.

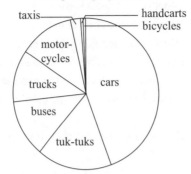

Traffic passing my home

a Which type of vehicle was most common?

b What percentage of the vehicles were tuk-tuks?

c How many trucks passed Jyoti's home?

d Which types of vehicles were least common?

6 In an exam the results for 120 students were: 5% attained an A grade, 12% attained a B grade, 41% attained a C grade, 25% attained a D grade and the rest attained E grade or lower.

a Represent this information on a pie chart.

b How many students attained an A?

c How many students attained a D or lower?

d Which grade was attained by most of the students?

Mixed exercise

1 Mika collected data about how many children different families in her community had. These are her results.

0	3	4	3	3	2	2	2	2	1	1	1
3	3	4	3	6	2	2	2	0	0	2	1
5	4	3	2	4	3	3	3	2	1	1	0
3	1	1	1	1	0	0	0	2	4	5	3

a How do you think Mika collected the data?

b Is this data discrete or continuous? Why?

c Is this data qualitative or quantitative? Why?

d Draw up a frequency table, with tallies, to organise the data.

e Represent the data on a pie chart.

f Draw a bar chart to compare the number of families that have three or fewer children with those that have four or more children.

2 The heights of a group of students are given in the table to the nearest centimetre.

Boys					Girls				
183	159	166	165	184	145	161	171	162	154
167	178	175	178	175	164	157	180	166	147
185	174	187	176	166	159	164	163	162	171

a Draw a back-to-back stem-and-leaf diagram to organise the data.

b How many students in total are taller than 170 cm?

c What does the diagram suggest about the heights of each group?

3 Mrs Sanchez bakes and sells cookies. One week she sells 420 peanut crunchies, 488 chocolate cups and 320 coconut munchies. Draw a pictogram to represent this data.

4 Study the chart in the margin.

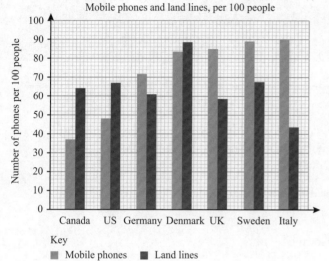

Mobile phones and land lines, per 100 people

Key
■ Mobile phones   ■ Land lines

a What do you call this type of chart?

b What does the chart show?

c Can you tell how many people in each country have a mobile phone from this chart? Explain your answer.

d In which countries do a greater proportion of the people have a land line than a mobile phone?

e In which countries do more people have mobile phones than land lines?

f In which country do more than 80% of the population have a land line and a mobile phone?

g What do you think the bars would look like for your country? Why?

5 Fractions and standard form

5.1 Equivalent fractions

- Equivalent means, 'has the same value'.
- To find equivalent fractions either multiply both the numerator and denominator by the same number or divide both the numerator and denominator by the same number.

You can cross multiply to make an equation and then solve it. For example:

$\dfrac{1}{2} \nearrow\!\!\!\!\swarrow \dfrac{x}{28}$

$2x = 28$

$x = 14$

Exercise 5.1

1 Write each fraction in its simplest form.

    a $\dfrac{6}{12}$ **b** $\dfrac{4}{12}$ **c** $\dfrac{3}{9}$ **d** $\dfrac{8}{32}$ **e** $\dfrac{12}{48}$

    f $\dfrac{125}{1000}$ **g** $\dfrac{3}{15}$ **h** $\dfrac{4}{6}$ **i** $\dfrac{24}{32}$ **j** $\dfrac{375}{1000}$

2 Find the missing value in each pair of equivalent fractions.

    a $\dfrac{3}{4} = \dfrac{x}{44}$ **b** $\dfrac{1}{3} = \dfrac{x}{900}$ **c** $\dfrac{1}{2} = \dfrac{x}{50}$ **d** $\dfrac{2}{5} = \dfrac{26}{x}$ **e** $\dfrac{5}{7} = \dfrac{120}{x}$

    f $\dfrac{6}{5} = \dfrac{66}{x}$ **g** $\dfrac{11}{9} = \dfrac{143}{x}$ **h** $\dfrac{5}{3} = \dfrac{80}{x}$ **i** $\dfrac{8}{12} = \dfrac{x}{156}$ **j** $\dfrac{7}{9} = \dfrac{49}{x}$

5.2 Operations on fractions

- To multiply fractions, multiply numerators by numerators and denominators by denominators. Mixed numbers should be rewritten as improper fractions before multiplying or dividing.
- To add or subtract fractions change them to equivalent fractions with the same denominator, then add (or subtract) the numerators only.
- To divide one fraction by another you multiply the first fraction by the reciprocal of the second fraction. (Any value multiplied by its reciprocal is 1). In plain language this means that you invert the second fraction (turn it upside down) and change the ÷ sign to a × sign.
- Unless you are specifically asked for a mixed number, give answers to calculations with fractions as proper or improper fractions in their simplest form.

! Tip

If you can simplify the fraction part first you will have smaller numbers to multiply to get the improper fraction.

Exercise 5.2

1 Rewrite each mixed number as an improper fraction in its simplest form.

    a $2\dfrac{7}{42}$ **b** $3\dfrac{5}{40}$ **c** $1\dfrac{12}{22}$ **d** $9\dfrac{30}{100}$ **e** $11\dfrac{24}{30}$

    f $3\dfrac{75}{100}$ **g** $14\dfrac{3}{4}$ **h** $2\dfrac{35}{45}$ **i** $9\dfrac{15}{45}$ **j** $-2\dfrac{7}{9}$

Remember, you can cancel to simplify when you are multiplying fractions.

2 Multiply, giving your answers in simplest form.

a $\frac{1}{5} \times \frac{3}{15}$ **b** $\frac{1}{4} \times \frac{2}{5}$ **c** $\frac{2}{3} \times \frac{6}{10}$ **d** $\frac{3}{5} \times \frac{9}{12}$ **e** $\frac{2}{11} \times \frac{8}{9}$

f $\frac{6}{11} \times \frac{2}{3}$ **g** $\frac{10}{13} \times \frac{3}{7}$ **h** $\frac{20}{50} \times \frac{9}{15}$ **i** $\frac{10}{14} \times \frac{3}{4}$ **j** $\frac{6}{8} \times \frac{3}{11}$

Remember, the word 'of' means ×.

3 Calculate.

a $1\frac{4}{5} \times 12$ **b** $\frac{9}{13} \times 7$ **c** $3\frac{1}{2} \times 4$ **d** $2\frac{1}{3} \times 2\frac{2}{5}$

e $2 \times 4\frac{1}{2} \times \frac{1}{3}$ **f** $\frac{1}{5} \times \frac{12}{19} \times 2\frac{1}{2}$ **g** $\frac{1}{3}$ of 360 **h** $\frac{3}{4}$ of $\frac{2}{7}$

i $\frac{8}{9}$ of 81 **j** $\frac{2}{3}$ of $4\frac{1}{2}$ **k** $\frac{1}{2}$ of $9\frac{16}{50}$ **l** $\frac{3}{4}$ of $2\frac{1}{3}$

! Tip

You can use any common denominator but it is easier to simplify if you use the lowest one.

4 Calculate, giving your answer as a fraction in simplest form.

a $\frac{3}{4} - \frac{1}{5}$ **b** $\frac{1}{5} + \frac{1}{6}$ **c** $\frac{1}{5} - \frac{1}{9}$ **d** $\frac{1}{6} + \frac{3}{8}$

e $\frac{2}{3} - \frac{4}{10}$ **f** $\frac{9}{10} - \frac{7}{12}$ **g** $\frac{4}{7} + \frac{1}{3}$ **h** $\frac{2}{3} + \frac{2}{5}$

i $\frac{7}{8} - \frac{1}{3}$ **j** $2\frac{1}{2} + 3\frac{1}{3}$ **k** $2\frac{1}{8} + 1\frac{1}{7}$ **l** $4\frac{3}{10} + 3\frac{3}{4}$

m $1\frac{1}{13} - \frac{4}{5}$ **n** $3\frac{9}{10} - 2\frac{7}{8}$ **o** $2\frac{5}{7} - 1\frac{1}{3}$ **p** $1\frac{1}{2} - \frac{7}{3}$

q $2\frac{1}{3} - \frac{17}{3}$ **r** $1\frac{4}{9} - \frac{13}{3}$ **s** $2\frac{1}{3} - \frac{12}{7}$ **t** $9\frac{1}{4} - \frac{17}{3}$

5 Calculate.

a $8 \div \frac{1}{3}$ **b** $12 \div \frac{7}{8}$ **c** $\frac{7}{8} \div 12$

d $\frac{2}{9} \div \frac{18}{30}$ **e** $\frac{8}{9} \div \frac{4}{5}$ **f** $1\frac{3}{7} \div 2\frac{2}{9}$

◀ REWIND

The order of operations rules (BODMAS) that were covered in chapter 1 apply here too. ◀

6 Simplify the following.

a $4 + \frac{2}{3} \times \frac{1}{3}$ **b** $2\frac{1}{8} - \left(2\frac{1}{5} - \frac{7}{8}\right)$ **c** $\frac{3}{7} \times \left(\frac{2}{3} + 6 \div \frac{2}{3}\right) + 5 \times \frac{2}{7}$

d $2\frac{7}{8} + \left(8\frac{1}{4} - 6\frac{3}{8}\right)$ **e** $\frac{5}{6} \times \frac{1}{4} + \frac{5}{8} \times \frac{1}{3}$ **f** $\left(5 \div \frac{3}{11} - \frac{5}{12}\right) \times \frac{1}{6}$

g $\left(\frac{5}{8} \div \frac{15}{4}\right) - \left(\frac{5}{6} \times \frac{1}{5}\right)$ **h** $\left(2\frac{2}{3} \div 4 - \frac{3}{10}\right) \times \frac{3}{17}$ **i** $\left(7 \div \frac{2}{9} - \frac{1}{3}\right) \times \frac{2}{3}$

7 Mrs West has \$900 dollars in her account. She spends $\frac{7}{12}$ of this.

     a How much does she spend?

     b How much does she have left?

8 It takes a builder $\frac{3}{4}$ of an hour to lay 50 tiles.

     a How many tiles will he lay in $4\frac{1}{2}$ hours?

     b If the builder lays tiles at the same rate for $6\frac{3}{4}$ hours a day, five days a week, how many tiles will he lay during the week?

5.3 Percentages

- Per cent means per hundred. A percentage is a fraction with a denominator of 100.
- To write one quantity as a percentage of another, express it as a fraction and then convert to a percentage by multiplying by 100.
- To find a percentage of a quantity, multiply the percentage by the quantity.
- To increase or decrease an amount by a percentage, find the percentage amount and add or subtract it from the original amount.

Exercise 5.3 A

1 Express the following as percentages. Round your answers to one decimal place.

a $\frac{1}{2}$ b $\frac{2}{3}$ c $\frac{1}{6}$ d $\frac{5}{8}$ e $\frac{93}{312}$

f 0.3   g 0.04   h 0.47   i 1.12   j 2.07

2 Express the following percentages as common fractions in their simplest form.

a 25%   b 80%   c 90%   d 12.5%
e 50%   f 98%   g 60%   h 22%

> **Tip**
>
> When finding a percentage of a quantity, your answer will have a unit and not a percentage sign because you are working out an amount.

3 Calculate.

a 30% of 200 kg   b 40% of $60   c 25% of 600 litres   d 22% of 250 ml
e 50% of $128   f 65% of $30   g 15% of 120 km   h 0.5% of 40 grams
i 2.6% of $80   j 9.5% of 5000 m³   k 2.5% of $80   l 120% of 3.5 kg

4 Calculate the percentage increase or decrease and copy and complete the table. Round your answers to one decimal place.

	Original amount	New amount	Percentage increase or decrease
a	40	48	
b	4000	3600	
c	1.5	2.3	
d	12 000	12 400	
e	12 000	8600	
f	9.6	12.8	
g	90	2400	

5 Increase each amount by the given percentage.

a $48 increased by 14%   b $700 increased by 35%
c $30 increased by 7.6%   d $40 000 increased by 0.59%
e $90 increased by 9.5%   f $80 increased by 24.6%

6 Decrease each amount by the given percentage.

    a $68 decreased by 14%   **b** $800 decreased by 35%

    c $90 decreased by 7.6%   **d** $20 000 decreased by 0.59%

    e $85 decreased by 9.5%   **f** $60 decreased by 24.6%

Exercise 5.3 B

1 75 250 tickets were available for an international cricket match. 62% of the tickets were sold within a day. How many tickets are left?

2 Mrs Rajah owns 15% of a company. If the company issues 12 000 shares, how many shares should she get?

3 A building, which cost $125 000 to build, increased in value by $3\frac{1}{2}$ %. What is the building worth now?

4 A player scored 18 out of the 82 points in a basketball match. What percentage of the points did he score?

5 A company has a budget of $24 000 for printing brochures. The marketing department has spent 34.6% of the budget already. How much money is left in the budget?

6 Josh currently earns $6000 per month. If he receives an increase of 3.8%, what will his new monthly earnings be?

7 A company advertises that its cottage cheese is 99.5% fat free. If this is correct, how many grams of fat would there be in a 500 gram tub of the cottage cheese?

8 Sally earns $25 per shift. Her boss says she can either have $7 more per shift or a 20% increase. Which is the better offer?

5.4 Standard form

- A number in standard form is written as: a number $\geqslant$ 1 but < 10 multiplied by 10 raised to a power.
- Standard form is also called scientific notation.
- To write a number in standard form:
  - first, place a decimal point after the first significant digit
  - then, count the number of place orders the first significant digits has to move to get from this new number to the original number, this gives the power of 10
  - finally, if the significant digit has moved to the left from the new number to get to the original (note this *looks* like the decimal point has moved to the right), has moved to the 10, the power of 10 is positive, but if the significant digit has moved to the right (or decimal to the left), the power of 10 is negative.
- To write a number in standard form as an ordinary number, multiply the decimal fraction by 10 to the given power.

> **! Tip**
> Make sure you know how your calculator deals with standard form.

Exercise 5.4 A

1 Write the following numbers in standard form.

    a 45 000   **b** 800 000   **c** 80   **d** 2 345 000

    e 4 190 000   **f** 32 000 000 000 **g** 0.0065   **h** 0.009

    i 0.00045   **j** 0.0000008   **k** 0.00675   **l** 0.00000000045

If the number part of your standard form answer is a whole number, there is no need to add a decimal point.

2 Write the following as ordinary numbers.

   a 2.5×10^3 **b** 3.9×10^4 **c** 4.265×10^5 **d** 1.045×10^{-5}

   e 9.15×10^{-6} **f** 1×10^{-9} **g** 2.8×10^{-5} **h** 9.4×10^7

   i 2.45×10^{-3}

◀ REWIND

Remember, the first significant figure is the first non-zero digit from the left. ◀

Exercise 5.4 B

1 Calculate, giving your answers in standard form correct to three significant figures.

   a 4216^6 **b** $(0.00009)^4$ **c** $0.0002 \div 2500^3$

   d $65\,000\,000 \div 0.0000045$ **e** $(0.0029)^3 \times (0.00365)^5$ **f** $(48 \times 987)^4$

   g $\dfrac{4525 \times 8760}{0.00002}$ **h** $\dfrac{9500}{0.0005^4}$ **i** $\sqrt{5.25} \times 10^8$

2 Simplify each of the following. Give your answer in standard form.

   a $(3 \times 10^{12}) \times (4 \times 10^{18})$ **b** $(1.5 \times 10^6) \times (3 \times 10^5)$ **c** $(1.5 \times 10^{12})^3$

   d $(1.2 \times 10^{-5}) \times (1.1 \times 10^{-6})$ **e** $(0.4 \times 10^{15}) \times (0.5 \times 10^{12})$ **f** $(8 \times 10^{17}) \div (3 \times 10^{12})$

   g $(1.44 \times 10^8) \div (1.2 \times 10^6)$ **h** $(8 \times 10^{-15}) \div (4 \times 10^{-12})$ **i** $\sqrt[3]{9.1} \times 10^{-8}$

3 The Sun has a mass of approximately 1.998×10^{27} tonnes. The planet Mercury has a mass of approximately 3.302×10^{20} tonnes.

   a Which has the greater mass?

   b How many times heavier is the greater mass compared with the smaller mass?

4 Light travels at a speed of 3×10^8 metres per second. The Earth is an average distance of 1.5×10^{11} m from the Sun and Pluto is an average 5.9×10^{12} m from the Sun.

   a Work out how long it takes light from the Sun to reach Earth (in seconds). Give your answer in both ordinary numbers and standard form.

   b How much longer does it take for the light to reach Pluto? Give your answer in both ordinary numbers and standard form.

5.5 Estimation

- Estimating involves rounding values in a calculation to numbers that are easy to work with (usually without the need for a calculator).
- An estimate allows you to check that your calculations make sense.

Exercise 5.5

Remember, the symbol ≈ means 'is approximately equal to'.

1 Use whole numbers to show why these estimates are correct.

   a $3.9 \times 5.1 \approx 20$ **b** $68 \times 5.03 \approx 350$ **c** $999 \times 6.9 \approx 7000$ **d** $42.02 \div 5.96 \approx 7$

2 Estimate the answers to each of these calculations to the nearest whole number.

   a $5.2 + 16.9 - 8.9 + 7.1$ **b** $(23.86 + 9.07) \div (15.99 - 4.59)$

   c $\dfrac{9.3 \times 7.6}{5.9 \times 0.95}$ **d** $8.9^2 \times \sqrt{8.98}$

Mixed exercise

1 Estimate the answer to each of these calculations to the nearest whole number.

   a 9.75×4.108 **b** $0.0387 \div 0.00732$ **c** $\dfrac{36.4 \times 6.32}{9.987}$ **d** $\sqrt{64.25} \times 3.098^2$

2 Simplify.

   a $\dfrac{160}{200}$ **b** $\dfrac{48}{72}$ **c** $\dfrac{36}{54}$

3 Calculate.

   a $\dfrac{4}{9} \times \dfrac{3}{8}$ **b** $84 \times \dfrac{3}{4}$ **c** $\dfrac{5}{9} \div \dfrac{1}{3}$ **d** $\dfrac{4}{15} + \dfrac{9}{15}$ **e** $\dfrac{9}{11} - \dfrac{3}{4}$

   f $\dfrac{5}{24} + \dfrac{7}{16}$ **g** $2\dfrac{1}{3} + 9\dfrac{1}{2}$ **h** $\left(4\dfrac{3}{4}\right)^2$ **i** $9\dfrac{1}{5} - 1\dfrac{7}{9}$

4 A family spends $\dfrac{1}{4}$ of their income on insurance and medical expenses, $\dfrac{1}{3}$ on living expenses and $\dfrac{1}{6}$ on savings. What fraction is left over?

5 Express the first quantity as a percentage of the second.

   a $400, $5000   **b** 4.8, 96   **c** 19, 30

6 A traffic officer pulls over 12 drivers at random from 450 passing cars. What percentage of drivers is this?

7 Find:

   a 30% of 82 kg   **b** 2.5% of 20 litres   **c** 17.5% of $400.

8 Express the following as percentages.

   a $\dfrac{1}{8}$ **b** $\dfrac{1}{3}$ **c** 425 out of 1250

9 Increase $90 by 15%.

10 Decrease $42.50 by 12%.

11 A baby weighed 3.25 kg when she was born. After 12 weeks, her mass had increased to 5.45 kg. Express this as a percentage increase, correct to one decimal place.

12 An aeroplane was flying at a height of 10 500 m when one engine failed. The plane dropped 28% in height. How many metres did it drop?

13 Joshua is paid $20.45 per hour. He normally works a 38-hour week.

   a Estimate his weekly earnings to the nearest dollar.
   b Estimate his annual earnings.

14 Pluto is 5.9×10^{12} m from the Sun.

   a Express this in kilometres, giving your answer in standard form.
   b In a certain position, the Earth is 1.47×10^8 km from the Sun. If Pluto, the Earth and the Sun are in a straight line in this position (and both planets are the same side of the Sun), calculate the approximate distance, in km, between the Earth and Pluto. Give your answer in standard form.

6 Equations and rearranging formulae

6.1 Further expansions of brackets

- Expand means to remove the brackets by multiplying out.
- Each term inside the bracket must be multiplied by the term outside the bracket.
- Negative terms in front of the brackets will affect the signs of the expanded terms.

Remember:

$+ \times - = -$

$- \times + = -$

$+ \times + = +$

$- + - = +$

Exercise 6.1

1 Expand and simplify if possible.

a $-2(x+y)$

b $-5(a-b)$

c $-3(-2x+y)$

d $2x(4-2y)$

e $-2x(x+3y)$

f $-9(x-1)$

g $3(4-2a)$

h $3-(4x+y)$

i $2x-(2x-3)$

j $-(3x+7)$

k $2x(x-y)$

l $-3x(x-2y)$

2 Expand and simplify as far as possible.

a $2(x-y)+3x(4-3)$

b $-4x(y-3)-(2x+xy)$

c $-2(x+3y)-2x(y-4)$

d $-\dfrac{1}{2}x(4-2y)-2y(3+x)$

e $12xy-(2+y)-3(4-x)$

f $2x^2(2-2y)-y(3-2x^2)$

g $-\dfrac{1}{4}x(4x-8)+2-(x^2-3)$

h $-2(x^2-2y)+4x(2x-2y)$

i $-\dfrac{1}{2}(8x-2)+3-(x+7)$

6.2 Solving linear equations

- To solve an equation, you find the value of the unknown letter (variable) that makes the equation true.
- If you add or subtract the same number (or term) to both sides of the equation, you produce an equivalent equation and the solution remains unchanged.
- If you multiply or divide each term on both sides of the equation by the same number (or term), you produce an equivalent equation and the solution remains unchanged.

Exercise 6.2

In this exercise leave answers as fractions rather than decimals, where necessary.

1 Solve these equations.

a $x+5=21$

b $x-10=14$

c $4x=32$

d $\dfrac{x}{6}=9$

e $9x=63$

f $x-2=-4$

g $x+7=-9$

h $\dfrac{x}{5}=-12$

i $x-4=-13$

j $-4x=60$

k $-2x=-26$

l $-3x=-45$

2 Solve these equations for x. Show the steps in your working.

a $2x+3=19$ **b** $3x-9=36$ **c** $2x+9=4$

d $4-2x=24$ **e** $-4x+5=21$ **f** $-2x-9=15$

3 Solve these equations for x. Show the steps in your working.

The variable can appear on both sides of the equation. You can add or subtract variables to both sides just like numbers.

a $2x+7=3x+4$ **b** $4x+6=x+18$ **c** $5x-2=3x+7$ **d** $9x-5=7x+3$

e $11x-4=x+32$ **f** $2x-1=14-x$ **g** $20-4x=5x+2$ **h** $3+4x=2x-7$

i $4x+5=7x-7$ **j** $2x-6=4x-3$ **k** $3x+2=5x-9$ **l** $x+9=5x-3$

4 Solve these equations for x.

a $3(x-2)=24$ **b** $5(x+4)=10$ **c** $3(3x+10)=6$ **d** $3(2x-1)=5$

e $-3(x-6)=-6$ **f** $4(3-5x)=7$ **g** $4(x+3)=x$ **h** $6(x+3)=4x$

When an equation has brackets it is usually best to expand them first.

i $3x+2=2(x-4)$ **j** $x-3=2(x+5)$ **k** $4(x+7)-3(x-5)=9$

l $2(x-1)-7(3x-2)=7(x-4)$

5 Solve these equations for x.

To remove the denominators of fractions in an equation, multiply each term on both sides by the common denominator.

a $\dfrac{x}{2}-3=6$ **b** $\dfrac{x}{3}+2=11$ **c** $\dfrac{4x}{6}=16$ **d** $\dfrac{28-x}{6}=12$

e $\dfrac{x-2}{3}=5$ **f** $\dfrac{x+3}{2}=16$ **g** $\dfrac{2x+5}{3}=9$ **h** $\dfrac{12x-1}{5}=9$

i $\dfrac{5x+2}{3}=-1$ **j** $\dfrac{5-2x}{4}=-1$ **k** $\dfrac{2x-1}{5}=x$ **l** $\dfrac{2x-3}{5}=x-6$

m $\dfrac{10x+2}{3}=6-x$ **n** $\dfrac{x}{2}-\dfrac{x}{5}=3$ **o** $\dfrac{2x}{3}-\dfrac{x}{2}=7$ **p** $-2\dfrac{(x+4)}{2}=x+7$

6.3 Factorising algebraic expressions

- The first step in factorising is to identify and 'take out' ALL common factors.
- Common factors can be numbers, variables, brackets or a combination of these.
- Factorising is the opposite of expanding – when you factorise you put brackets back into the expression.

Exercise 6.3

Remember, x^2 means $x \times x$, so x is a factor of x^2

1 Find the highest common factor of each pair.

a $3x$ and 21 **b** 40 and $8x$ **c** $15a$ and $5b$

d $2a$ and ab **e** $3xy$ and $12yz$ **f** $5a^2b$ and $20ab^2$

g $8xy$ and $28xyz$ **h** $9pq$ and p^2q^2 **i** $14abc$ and $7a^2b$

j x^2y^3z and $2xy^2z^2$ **k** $2a^2b^4$ and ab^3 **l** $3x^3y^2$ and $15xy$

Find the HCF of the numbers first. Then find the HCF of the variables, if there is one, in alphabetical order.

2 Factorise as fully as possible.

a $12x+48$ **b** $2+8y$ **c** $4a-16$ **d** $2x-12$

e $4x-20$ **f** $16a-8$ **g** $3x-xy$ **h** $ab+5a$

i $3x-15y$ **j** $8a+24$ **k** $12x-18$ **l** $24xyz-8xz$

m $9ab-12bc$ **n** $6xy-4yz$ **o** $14x-26xy$ **p** $-14x^2-7x^5$

3 Factorise the following.

> Remember, if one of the terms is exactly the same as the common factor, you must put a 1 where the term would appear in the bracket.

a x^2+8x **b** $12a-a^2$ **c** $9x^2+4x$ **d** $22x-16x^2$

e $6ab^2+8b$ **f** $18xy-36x^2y$ **g** $6x-9x^2$ **h** $14x^2y^2-6xy^2$

i $9abc^3-3a^2b^2c^2$ **j** $4x^2-7xy$ **k** $3ab^2-4b^2c$ **l** $14a^2b-21ab^2$

4 Remove a common factor to factorise each of the following expressions.

a $x(3+y)+4(3+y)$ **b** $x(y-3)+5(y-3)$

c $3(a+2b)-2a(a+2b)$ **d** $4a(2a-b)-3(2a-b)$

e $x(2-y)+(2-y)$ **f** $x(x-3)+4(x-3)$

g $9(2+y)-x(y+2)$ **h** $4a(2b-c)-(c-2b)$

i $3x(x-6)-5(x-6)$ **j** $x(x-y)-(2x-2y)$

k $3x(2x+3)+y(3+2x)$ **l** $4(x-y)-x(3x-3y)$

6.4 Rearranging of a formula

- A formula is a general rule, usually involving several variables, for example, the area of a rectangle, $A=bh$.
- A variable is called the subject of the formula when it is on its own on one side of the equals sign.
- You can rearrange a formula to make any variable the subject. You use the same rules that you used to solve equations.

Exercise 6.4 A

1 Make m the subject if $D=km$

2 Make c the subject if $y=mx+c$

3 Given that $P=ab-c$, make b the subject of the formula.

4 Given that $a=bx+c$, make b the subject of the formula.

5 Make a the subject of each formula.

> **!** **Tip**
> Pay attention to the signs when you rearrange a formula.

a $a+b=c$ **b** $a-3b=2c$ **c** $ab-c=d$ **d** $ab+c=d$

e $bc-a=d$ **f** $bc-a=-d$ **g** $\dfrac{2a+b}{c}=d$ **h** $\dfrac{c+ba}{d}=e$

i $abc-d=e$ **j** $cab+d=ef$ **k** $\dfrac{ab}{c}+de=f$ **l** $c+\dfrac{ab}{d}=e$

m $c(a-b)=d$ **n** $d(a+2b)=c$

Exercise 6.4 B

1 The perimeter of a rectangle can be given as $P=2(l+b)$, where P is the perimeter, l is the length and b is the breadth.

a Make b the subject of the formula.

b Find b if the rectangle has a length of 45 cm and a perimeter of 161 cm.

Tip

If you are given a value for π, you must use the given value to avoid calculator and rounding errors.

Tip

In questions such as Q3, it may be helpful to draw a diagram to show what the parts of the formula represent.

2 The circumference of a circle can be found using the formula $C = 2\pi r$, where r is the radius of the circle.

  a Make r the subject of the formula.
  b Find the radius of a circle of circumference 56.52 cm. Use $\pi = 3.14$.
  c Find the diameter of a circle of circumference 144.44 cm. Use $\pi = 3.14$.

3 The area of a trapezium can be found using the formula $A = \dfrac{h(a+b)}{2}$, where h is the distance between the parallel sides and a and b are the lengths of the parallel sides. By transforming the formula and substitution, find the length of b, in a trapezium of area 9.45 cm² with $a = 2.5$ cm and $h = 3$ cm.

Mixed exercise

1 Solve for x.

  a $4x - 9 = -21$
  b $5x + 4 = -26$
  c $\dfrac{2x - 4}{7} = 2$
  d $5 = \dfrac{1 - 4x}{5}$

  e $4x - 6 = 12 - 5x$
  f $4x - 8 = 3(2x + 6)$
  g $\dfrac{3x - 7}{4} = \dfrac{1 - 4x}{8}$
  h $\dfrac{3(2x - 5)}{5} = \dfrac{x + 1}{2}$

2 Make x the subject of each formula.

  a $m = nxp - r$
  b $m = \dfrac{nx + p}{q}$

3 Expand and simplify where possible.

Remember to inspect your answer to see if there are any like terms. If there are, add and/or subtract them to simplify the expression.

  a $3(x - 1) + 5$
  b $-4x(3x - 2)$
  c $-2(4x - 2y + 3)$
  d $-2y(7 - y) - 2y$
  e $4(2x - 1) + 3(x + 3)$
  f $x(5x - 1) + 2(4x - 2)$
  g $-2x(x - 4) + 3x$
  h $6x(2x + 3) - 2x(x - 3)$

4 Factorise fully.

  a $4x - 8$
  b $12x - 3y$
  c $-2x - 4$
  d $3xy - 24x$
  e $14x^2y^2 + 7xy$
  f $2(x - y) + x(x - y)$
  g $x(4 + 3x) - 3(3x + 4)$
  h $4x^2(x + y) - 8x(x + y)$

5 Given that, for a rectangle, area = length × breadth, write an expression for the area of each rectangle. Expand each expression fully.

a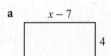

b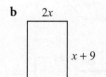

c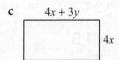

d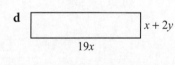

7 Perimeter, area and volume

7.1 Perimeter and area in two dimensions

- Perimeter is the total distance around the outside of a shape. You can find the perimeter of any shape by adding up the lengths of the sides.
- The perimeter of a circle is called the circumference. Use the formula $C = \pi d$ or $C = 2\pi r$ to find the circumference of a circle.
- Area is the total space contained within a shape. Use these formulae to calculate the area of different shapes:
  - triangle: $A = \dfrac{bh}{2}$
  - square: $A = s^2$
  - rectangle: $A = bh$
  - parallelogram: $A = bh$
  - rhombus: $A = bh$
  - kite: $A = \dfrac{1}{2}(\text{product of diagonals})$
  - trapezium: $A = \dfrac{(\text{sum of parallel sides})h}{2}$
  - circle: $A = \pi r^2$
- You can work out the area of complex shapes in a few steps. Divide complex shapes into known shapes. Work out the area of each part and then add the areas together to find the total area.

Exercise 7.1 A

1 Find the perimeter of each shape.

a
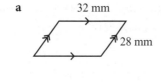
32 mm
28 mm

b
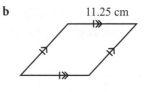
11.25 cm

c
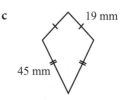
19 mm
45 mm

d
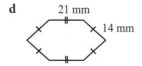
21 mm
14 mm

e
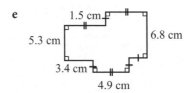
1.5 cm
5.3 cm
6.8 cm
3.4 cm
4.9 cm

f
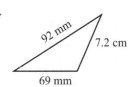
92 mm
7.2 cm
69 mm

2 Find the perimeter of each of these shapes. Give your answers correct to two decimal places.

a 5 m

b 7 cm

c 21 mm

d 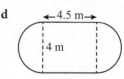 4.5 m, 4 m

e 3 m

f 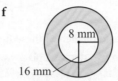 8 mm, 16 mm

g 60°, 8 cm

3 A square field has a perimeter of 360 m. What is the length of one of its sides?

4 Find the cost of fencing a rectangular plot 45 m long and 37 m wide if the cost of fencing is $45.50 per metre.

5 An isosceles triangle has a perimeter of 28 cm. Calculate the length of each of the equal sides if the remaining side is 100 mm long.

6 How much string would you need to form a circular loop with a diameter of 28 cm?

7 The rim of a bicycle wheel has a radius of 31.5 cm.

　a What is the circumference of the rim? Give your answer as an exact multiple of π.

　b The tyre that goes onto the rim is 3.5 cm thick. Calculate the circumference of the wheel when the tyre is fitted to it. Give your answer as an exact multiple of π.

Exercise 7.1 B

1 Find the area of each of these shapes.

a 29 mm

b 14 m 29 m

c 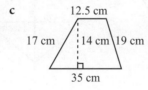 12.5 cm, 17 cm, 14 cm, 19 cm, 35 cm

d 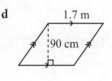 1.7 m, 90 cm

e 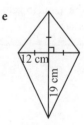 12 cm, 19 cm

f 21 cm 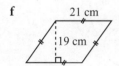 19 cm

g 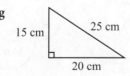 15 cm, 25 cm, 20 cm

h 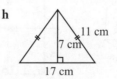 11 cm, 7 cm, 17 cm

i 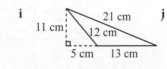 11 cm, 21 cm, 12 cm, 5 cm, 13 cm

j 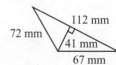 112 mm, 72 mm, 41 mm, 67 mm

k 2.4 m

l 147.6 cm 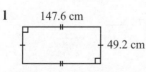 49.2 cm

m 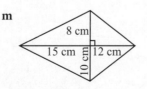 8 cm, 15 cm, 12 cm, 10 cm

2 Find the area of each shape. Give your answers correct to two decimal places.

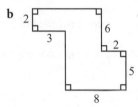

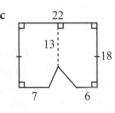

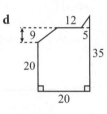

3 Find the area of each of these figures. Show your working clearly in each case and give your answers to two decimal places where necessary. All dimensions are given in centimetres.

> **Tip**
> Work out any missing dimensions on the figure using the given dimensions and the properties of shapes.

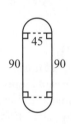

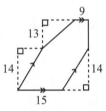

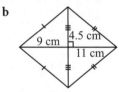

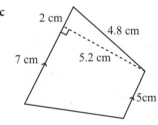

4 Find the area of the following figures giving your answers correct to two decimal places. (Give your answer in terms of π for part (**f**).)

> **Tip**
> Divide irregular shapes into known shapes and combine the areas to get the total area.

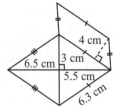

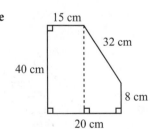

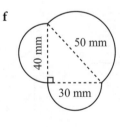

Draw a diagram and add all the information you are given.

5 A 1.5 m × 2.4 m rectangular rug is placed on the floor in a 3.5 m × 4.2 m rectangular room. How much of the floor is not covered by the rug?

6 The area of a rhombus of side 8 cm is 5600 mm². Determine the height of the rhombus.

Exercise 7.1 C

1 Calculate the length of the arc *AB*, subtended by the given angle, in each of these circles. Give your answers correct to two decimal places.

a
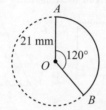

b
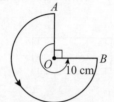

c

2 The diagram shows a cross-section of the Earth. Two cities, *X* and *Y*, lie on the same longitude. Given that the radius of the Earth is 6371 km, calculate the distance, *XY*, between the two cities. Give your answer correct to two decimal places.

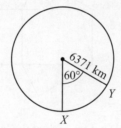

3 Calculate the shaded area of each circle. Give your answers as a multiple of π.

a
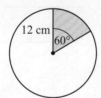

b
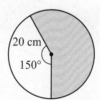

c

4 A large circular pizza has a diameter of 25 cm. The pizza restaurant cuts its pizzas into eight equal slices. Calculate the size of each slice in cm² correct to three significant figures.

7.2 Three-dimensional objects

- Any solid object is three-dimensional. The three dimensions of a solid are length, breadth and height.
- The net of a solid is a two-dimensional diagram. It shows the shape of all faces of the solid and how they are attached to each other. If you fold up a net, you get a model of the solid.

Exercise 7.2

1 Which solids would be made from the following faces?

a
× 6

b
× 2   × 2   × 2

c
× 4   × 1

d
× 8

2 Describe the solid you could produce using each of the following nets.

a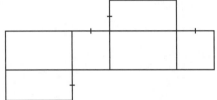

b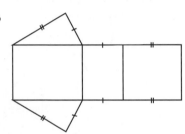

c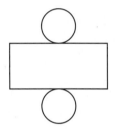

3 Sketch a possible net for each of the following solids.

a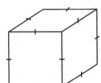

b

c

d

7.3 Surface areas and volumes of solids

- The surface area of a three-dimensional object is the total area of all its faces.
- The volume of a three-dimensional object is the amount of space it occupies.
- You can find the volume of a cube or cuboid using the formula $V = l \times b \times h$, where l is the length, b is the breadth and h is the height of the object.
- A prism is a three-dimensional object with a uniform cross-section, (the end faces of the solid are identical and parallel). If you slice through the prism anywhere along its length (and parallel to the end faces), you will get a section the same shape and size as the end faces. Cubes, cuboids and cylinders are examples of prisms.
- You can find the volume of any prism (including a cylinder) by multiplying the area of its cross-section by the distance between the parallel faces. This is expressed in the formula $V = al$, where a is the area of the base and l is the length of the prism. You need to use the appropriate area formula for the shape of the cross-section.
- Find the volume of a cone using the formula, $V = \frac{1}{3}\pi r^2 h$, where h is the perpendicular height. To find the curved surface area use the formula, surface area $= \pi r l$, where l is the slant height of the cone.
- Find the volume of a pyramid using the formula, $V = \dfrac{\text{area of base} \times h}{3}$, where h is the perpendicular height.
- Find the volume of a sphere using the formula, $V = \frac{4}{3}\pi r^3$. To find the surface area use the formula, surface area $= 4\pi r^2$.

Exercise 7.3

Tip
Drawing the nets of the shapes may help you work out the area of each face.

1 Calculate the surface area of each shape. Give your answers to two decimal places where necessary.

a
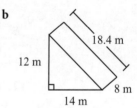
0.5 mm
0.4 mm
1.2 mm

b
18.4 m
12 m
14 m
8 m

c
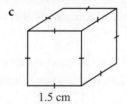
1.5 cm

d
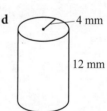
4 mm
12 mm

2 A wooden cube has six identical square faces, each of area 64 cm².

   a What is the surface area of the cube?
   b What is the height of the cube?

3 Mrs Nini is ordering wooden blocks to use in her maths classroom. The blocks are cuboids with dimensions 10 cm × 8 cm × 5 cm.

   a Calculate the surface area of one block.
   b Mrs Nini needs 450 blocks. What is the total surface area of all the blocks?
   c She decides to varnish the blocks. A tin of varnish covers an area of 4 m².
      How many tins will she need to varnish all the blocks?

Remember,
1 m² = 10 000 cm²

Tip

The length of the prism is the distance between the two parallel faces. When a prism is turned onto its face, the length may look like a height. Work out the area of the cross-section (end face) before you apply the volume formula.

4 Calculate the volume of each prism. Give your answers to two decimal places where necessary.

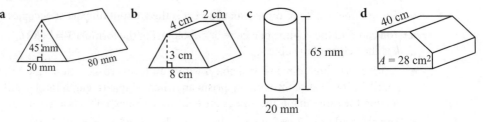

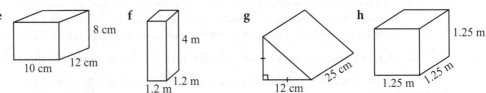

5 Find the volume of the following solids. Give your answers correct to two decimal places.

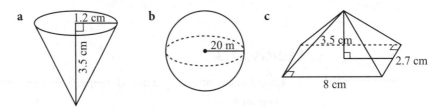

6 A pocket dictionary is 14 cm long, 9.5 cm wide and 2.5 cm thick. Calculate the volume of space it takes up.

7 a Find the volume of a lecture room that is 8 m long, 8 m wide and 3.5 m high.

   b Safety regulations state that during an hour long lecture each person in the room must have 5 m³ of air. Calculate the maximum number of people who can attend an hour long lecture.

8 A cylindrical tank is 30 m high with an inner radius of 150 cm. Calculate how much water the tank will hold when full. Give your answer in terms of π.

9 A machine shop has four different rectangular prisms of volume 64 000 mm³. Copy and fill in the possible dimensions for each prism to complete the table.

Volume (mm³)	64 000	64 000	64 000	64 000
Length (mm)	80	50		
Breadth (mm)	40		80	
Height (mm)				16

Mixed exercise

1 A circular plate on a stove has a diameter of 21 cm. There is a metal strip around the outside of the plate.

   a Calculate the surface area of the top of the plate.
   b Calculate the length of the metal strip.

2 What is the radius of a circle with an area of 65 cm²?

3 Calculate the shaded area in each figure. Give your answers to two decimal places where necessary.

a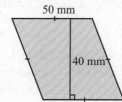

b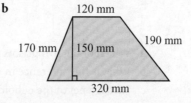

c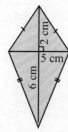

d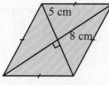

e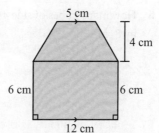

f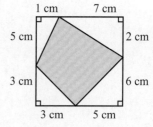

g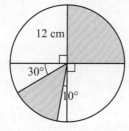

Tip

If a shape has a piece cut out of it, the perimeter includes the inner and outer boundaries of the shape.

4 *MNOP* is a trapezium with an area of 150 cm². Calculate the length of *NO*.

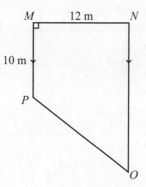

5 Study the two prisms.

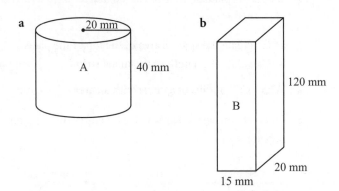

a

b

a Which of the two prisms has the smaller volume?

b What is the difference in volume? Give your answer correct to two decimal places.

c Sketch a net of the cuboid. Your net does not need to be to scale, but you must indicate the dimensions of each face on the net.

d Calculate the surface area of each prism. Give your answer to two decimal places where necessary.

6 How many cubes of side 4 cm can be packed into a wooden box measuring 32 cm by 16 cm by 8 cm?

Introduction to probability

8.1 Basic probability

- Probability is a measure of the chance that something will happen. It is measured on a scale of 0 to 1:
  - outcomes with a probability of 0 are impossible
  - outcomes with a probability of 1 are certain
  - an outcome with a probability of 0.5 or $\frac{1}{2}$ has an even chance of occurring.
- Probabilities can be found through doing an experiment, such as tossing a coin. Each time you perform the experiment is called a trial. If you want to get heads, then heads is your desired outcome or successful outcome.
- To calculate probability from the outcomes of experiments, use the formula:

$$\text{Experimental probability of outcome} = \frac{\text{number of successful outcomes}}{\text{number of trials}}$$

- Experimental probability is also called the relative frequency.

Exercise 8.1

P(A), P(B), etc., are often used to express the probability of outcome A, B, etc. For example, the experimental probability of getting a six when you roll a die would be expressed as P(6).

1 Salma has a bag containing one red, one white and one green ball. She draws a ball at random and replaces it before drawing again. She repeats this 50 times. She uses a tally table to record the outcomes of her experiment.

Red	ⅢⅠ ⅢⅠ ⅢⅠ
White	ⅢⅠ ⅢⅠ ⅢⅠ III
Green	ⅢⅠ ⅢⅠ ⅢⅠ II

a Calculate the relative frequency of drawing each colour.
b Express her chance of drawing a red ball as a percentage.
c What is the sum of the three relative frequencies?
d What should your chances be in theory of drawing each colour?

2 It is Josh's job to call customers who have had their car serviced at the dealer to check whether they are happy with the service they received. He kept this record of what happened for 200 calls made one month.

Result	Frequency
Spoke to customer	122
Phone not answered	44
Left message on answering machine	22
Phone engaged or out of order	10
Wrong number	2

a Calculate the relative frequency of each event as a decimal fraction.

b Is it highly likely, likely, unlikely or highly unlikely that the following outcomes will occur when Josh makes a call:

   i   the call will be answered by the customer
   ii   the call will be answered by a machine
   iii he will dial the wrong number

8.2 Theoretical probability

- You can calculate the theoretical probability of an event without doing experiments if the outcomes are equally likely. Use the formula:

$$P(\text{outcome}) = \frac{\text{number of favourable outcomes}}{\text{number of possible outcomes}}$$

  For example, when you toss a coin you can get heads or tails (two possible outcomes). The probability of heads is $P(H) = \frac{1}{2}$.

- You need to work out what *all* the possible outcomes are before you can calculate theoretical probability.

Tip

It is helpful to list the possible outcomes so that you know what to substitute in the formula.

Remember, 1 is NOT a prime number.

Exercise 8.2

1 A container has three red and three blue counters in it. A counter is drawn and its colour is noted.

   a What are the possible outcomes?
   b What is the probability of drawing a red counter?
   c Is it equally likely that you will draw red as blue?

2 An unbiased six-sided die with the numbers one to six on the faces is rolled.

   a What are the possible outcomes of this event?
   b Calculate the probability of rolling a prime number.
   c What is the probability of rolling an even number?
   d What is the probability of rolling a number greater than seven?

3 Sally has ten identical cards numbered one to ten. She draws a card at random and records the number on it.

   a What are the possible outcomes for this event?
   b Calculate the probability that Sally will draw:
      i   the number five   ii   any one of the ten numbers
      iii a multiple of three   iv   a number < 4
      v   a number < 5   vi   a number < 6
      vii a square number   viii a number < 10
      ix   a number > 10

4 There are five cups of coffee on a tray. Two of them contain sugar.

   a What are your chances of choosing a cup with sugar in it?
   b Which choice is most likely? Why?

5 Mike has four cards numbered one to four. He draws one card and records the number. Calculate the probability that the result will be:

   a a multiple of three   **b** a multiple of two   **c** factor of three

6 For a fly-fishing competition, the organisers place 45 trout, 30 salmon and 15 pike in a small dam.

   a What is an angler's chance of catching a salmon on her first attempt?

   b What is the probability she catches a trout?

   c If the dam already contained same salmon and trout such that the probability of catching one of each was $\frac{8}{21}$ and $\frac{10}{21}$ respectively. What is the probability of catching a pike if there are still only 15 in the dam?

7 A dartboard is divided into 20 sectors numbered from one to 20. If a dart is equally likely to land in any of these sectors, calculate:

   a P(<8)   **b** P(odd)   **c** P(prime)

   d P(multiple of 3)   **e** P(multiple of 5).

8 A school has forty classrooms numbered from one to 40. Work out the probability that a classroom number has the numeral '1' in it.

8.3 The probability that an event does not happen

- An event may happen or it may not happen. For example, you may throw a six when you roll a die, but you may not.
- The probability of an event happening may be different from the probability of the event not happening, but the two combined probabilities will always add up to one.
- If A is an event happening, then A′ (or $\overline{A}$) represents the event A not happening and P(A′) = 1 – P(A).

Exercise 8.3

1 The probability that a driver is speeding on a stretch of road is 0.27. What is the probability that a driver is not speeding?

2 The probability of drawing a green ball in an experiment is $\frac{3}{8}$. What is the probability of not drawing a green ball?

3 A container holds 300 sweets in five different flavours. The probability of choosing a particular flavour is given in the table.

Flavour	Strawberry	Lime	Lemon	Blackberry	Apple
P(flavour)	0.21	0.22	0.18	0.23	

   a Calculate P(apple).

   b What is P(not apple)?

   c Calculate the probability of choosing P(neither lemon nor lime)?

   d Calculate the number of each flavoured sweet in the packet.

4   In an opinion poll, 5000 teenagers were asked what make of mobile phone they would choose from four options (A, B, C or D). The probability of choosing each option is given in the table.

Phone	A	B	C	D
P(option)	0.36	0.12	0.4	

a   Calculate P(D).

b   What is P(D′)?

c   What is the probability a teenager would choose either B or D?

d   How many teenagers would you expect to choose option C if these probabilities are correct?

8.4   Possibility diagrams

- The set of all possible outcomes is called the sample space (or probability space) of an event.
- Possibility diagrams can be used to show all outcomes clearly.
- When you are dealing with combined events, it is much easier to find a probability if you represent the sample space in a diagram: possibility diagrams are useful for doing this.

Tip

Think of the probability space diagram as a map of all the possible outcomes in an experiment.

FAST FORWARD ▶

Tree diagrams are also probability space diagrams. These are dealt with in detail in chapter 24. ▶

Exercise 8.4

1   Draw a possibility diagram to show all possible outcomes when you toss two coins at the same time. Use your diagram to help you answer the following.

a   What is P(at least one tail)?

b   What is P(no tails)?

2   Jess has three green cards numbered one to three and three yellow cards also numbered one to three.

a   Draw a possibility diagram to show all possible outcomes when one green and one yellow card is chosen at random.

b   How many possible outcomes are there?

c   What is the probability that the number on both the cards will be the same?

d   What is the probability of getting a total < 4 if the scores on the cards are added?

3   Two normal six-sided dice are rolled. Find the probability of getting:

a   two 4s

b   a 4 and a 6

c   a total of 7

d   a total of 9

8.5 Combining independent and mutually exclusive events

- When one outcome in a trial has no effect on the next outcome we say the events are independent.
  - Drawing a counter at random from a bag, replacing it and then drawing another counter is an example of independent events. Because you replace the counter, the first draw does not affect the second draw.
- If A and B *are* independent events then: P(A happens and then B happens) = P(A) × P(B) or
P(A and B) = P(A) × P(B)
- Mutually exclusive events cannot happen at the same time.
  - For example, you cannot throw an odd number and an even number at the same time when you roll a die.
- If A and B *are* mutually exclusive events then: P(A or B) = P(A) + P(B)

Exercise 8.5

1 Nico is on a bus driving through Ohio and he is bored, so he amuses himself by choosing a consonant and a vowel at random from the names of towns on road signs. The next road sign is CALCUTTA.

 a Draw up a sample space diagram to show all the options that Nico has.
 b Calculate P(T and A).
 c Calculate P(C or L and U).
 d Calculate P(not L and U).

2 Ami has three tiles with the letters A, M and I on them and a coin. If she picks a letter at random and tosses the coin, what is the probability she will get the letter M and heads?

3 A box contains 4 green apples and 5 red apples. An apple is picked at random, replaced and then a second apple is picked at random. Work out the probability that:

 a both apples are green
 b both apples are red
 c one apple is green and one is red.

Mixed exercise

1   A coin is tossed a number of times giving the following results.

  Heads: 4083   Tails: 5917

  a How many times was the coin tossed?
  b Calculate the relative frequency of each outcome.
  c What is the probability that the next toss will result in heads?
  d Jess says she thinks the results show that the coin is biased. Do you agree? Give a reason for your answer.

2   A bag contains 10 red, eight green and two white counters. Each counter has an equal chance of being chosen. Calculate the probability of:

  a choosing a red ball
  b choosing a green ball
  c choosing a white ball
  d choosing a blue ball
  e choosing a red or a green ball
  f not choosing a white ball
  g choosing a ball that is not red

3   Two normal unbiased dice are rolled and the sum of the numbers on their faces is recorded.

  a Calculate P(12).
  b Which sum has the greatest probability? What is the probability of rolling this sum?
  c What is P(not even)?
  d What is P(sum < 5)?

4   Micah uses a computer to pick a random 5-digit positive integer. Work out the probability of choosing:

  a a number ending in 9
  b an odd number
  c a multiple of 5

5   Grace has two sets of cards. One set contains the letters B, T, L and M, the other contains the letters A, E and O.

  She picks a card at random from each set and puts them together, consonant first. Calculate the probability that she:

  a makes the word BE or ME
  b has the letter O in the combination
  c makes the word TEA
  d does not get a B or an E

9 Sequences and sets

9.1 Sequences

- A number sequence is a list of numbers that follows a set pattern. Each number in the sequence is called a term. T_1 is the first term, T_{10} is the tenth term and T_n is the nth term, or general term.
- A linear sequence has a constant difference (d) between the terms. The general rule for finding the nth term of any linear sequence is $T_n = a + (n-1)d$, where a is the first value in the sequence.
- When you know the rule for making a sequence, you can find the value of any term. Substitute the term number into the rule and solve it.

You should recognise these sequences of numbers:

square numbers: 1, 4, 9, 16 …
cube numbers: 1, 8, 27, 64 …
triangular numbers: 1, 3, 6, 10 …
Fibonacci numbers: 1, 1, 2, 3, 5, 8 …

Exercise 9.1

1 Find the next three terms in each sequence and describe the term-to-term rule.

    a 11, 13, 15 …   **b** 88, 99, 110 …   **c** 64, 32, 16 …   **d** 8, 16, 24, 32 …

    e $-2, -4, -6, -8$ …   **f** $\frac{1}{4}, \frac{1}{2}, 1$ …   **g** 1, 2, 4, 7 …   **h** 1, 6, 11, 16 …

2 List the first four terms of the sequences that follow these rules.

    a Start with seven and add two each time.

    b Start with 37 and subtract five each time.

    c Start with one and multiply by $\frac{1}{2}$ each time.

    d Start with five then multiply by two and add one each time.

    e Start with 100, divide by two and subtract three each time.

3 Write down the first three terms of each of these sequences. Then find the 35th term.

    a $T_n = 2n + 3$ **b** $T_n = n^2$ **c** $T_n = 6n - 1$ **d** $T_n = n^3 - 1$

    e $T_n = n^2 - n$ **f** $T_n = 3 - 2n$

4 Consider the sequence:

    2, 10, 18, 26, 34, 42, 50 …

    a Find the nth term of the sequence.

    b Find the 200th term.

    c Which term of this sequence has the value 234? Show full working.

    d Show that 139 is not a term in the sequence.

FAST FORWARD

You will work with sets of numbers again in Section 9.3. ▶

5 For each sequence below find the general term and the 50th term.

    a 7, 9, 11, 13 …   **b** $-5, -13, -21, -29$ …   **c** 2, 8, 14, 20, 26 …

    d 4, 9, 16, 25 …   **e** 2.3, 3.5, 4.7, 5.9 …

9.2 Rational and irrational numbers

- You can express any rational number as a fraction in the form of $\frac{a}{b}$ where a and b are integers and $b \neq 0$.
- Whole numbers, integers, common fractions, mixed numbers, terminating decimal fractions and recurring decimals are all rational.
- You can convert recurring decimal fractions into the form $\frac{a}{b}$.
- Irrational numbers cannot be written in the form $\frac{a}{b}$. Irrational numbers are all non-recurring, non-terminating decimals.
- The set of real numbers is made up of rational and irrational numbers.

In 1.$\dot{2}$, the dot above the two in the decimal part means it is recurring (the '2' repeats forever). If a set of numbers recurs, e.g. 0.273273273..., there will be a dot at the start and end of the recurring set: 0.$\dot{2}$7$\dot{3}$.

Exercise 9.2

1 Write down all the irrational numbers in each set of real numbers.

    a $\frac{3}{8}$, $\sqrt{16}$, $\sqrt[3]{16}$, $\frac{22}{7}$, $\sqrt{12}$, 0.090090009..., $\frac{31}{3}$, 0.020202...,

    b 23, $\sqrt{45}$, 0.$\dot{6}$, $\frac{3}{4}$, $\sqrt[3]{90}$, π, $5\frac{1}{2}$, $\sqrt{8}$, 0.834,

9.3 Sets

- A set is a list or collection of objects that share a characteristic.
- An element ($\in$) is a member of a set. The number of elements in any set, for example Set A, can be described as n(A).
- A universal set ($\mathscr{E}$) contains all the possible elements appropriate to a particular problem.
- The elements of two sets can be combined (without repeats) to form the union ($\cup$) of the two sets.
- The elements that two sets have in common is called the intersection ($\cap$) of the two sets.
- A Venn diagram is a pictorial method of showing sets.

Exercise 9.3 A

! Tip

Make sure you know the meaning of the symbols used to describe sets and parts of sets.

1 Say whether each of the following statements is true or false.

    a $2 \in$ {odd numbers}.
    b $8 \in$ {cubed numbers}.
    c $\{1, 2, 3\} \cap \{3, 6, 9\} = \{1, 2, 3, 6, 9\}$.
    d $\{1, 2, 3\} \cup \{3, 6, 9\} = \{1, 2, 3, 6, 9\}$.
    e $A = \{1, 2, 3\}$, $B = \{3, 6, 9\}$, so $A = B$.

Sometimes listing the elements of each set will make it easier to answer the questions.

2 $\mathscr{E} = $ {whole numbers from 1 to 20}, $A = $ {even numbers from 1 to 12}, $B = $ {odd numbers from 1 to 15} and $C = $ {multiples of 3 from 1 to 20}.
  List the elements of the following sets.

    a $A \cap B$
    b $B \cup C$

3 List the elements of the following sets.

    a $\{x : x \in$ integers, $-2 \leqslant x < 3\}$
    b $\{x : x \in$ natural numbers, $x \leqslant 5\}$

4 Given Set A = {odd numbers between 0 and 10} and Set B = {even numbers between 1 and 9}, find:

    a $A \cup B$ **b** $A \cap B$

Exercise 9.3 B

1 Draw a Venn diagram to show the following sets and write each element in its correct space.

    $\mathscr{E}$ = {letters in the alphabet}
    P = {letters in the word physics}
    C = {letters in the word chemistry}

2 Use the Venn diagram you drew in question 1 to find:

    a $n(C)$ **b** n(not in P)
    c $C \cap P$ **d** $P \cup C$

3 Make two copies of this Venn diagram and shade the following sets:

    a $A \cup C$
    b $A \cap B \cap C$.

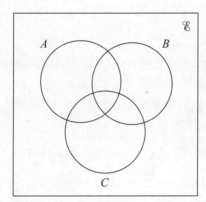

> **Tip**
> You can use any shapes to draw a Venn diagram but usually the universal set is drawn as a rectangle and circles within it show the sets.

4 $\mathscr{E}$ = {whole numbers from 1 to 10}
    A = {even numbers from 1 to 10}
    B = {multiples of five from 1 to 10}
    a Draw a Venn diagram to show the information.
    b Determine:
        i $A \cap B$ **ii** n(elements in $\mathscr{E}$ but not in A or B)
        iii $A \cup B$

5 You are told that $n(\mathscr{E})$ = 30, $n(A)$ = 18, $n(B)$ = 12 and $n(A \cap B)$ = 4.

    Draw a Venn diagram to show this information.

6 $\mathscr{E}$ = {x: x is a whole number from 1 to 20}

    Set A = {square numbers}

    Set B = {Factors of 12}

    Set C = {Multiples of 3}

a Copy and complete this Venn diagram.

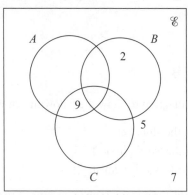

b List:

   i $A \cap B \cap C$ ii $A \cup B \cup C$

   iii Set D, such that it contains numbers that are in $\mathscr{E}$ but not in A, B or C.

Venn diagrams are useful for representing the information in problems involving sets of data where some of the data overlaps.

7 In a factory that makes T-shirts, 100 T-shirts were quality tested and it was found that 12 had flaws in the printed logos and 15 had flaws in the stitching. 4 T-shirts had both flaws.

   a How many T-shirts had at least one flaw?

   b How many T-shirts had no flaws?

Mixed exercise

1 For each of the following sequences, find the nth term and the 120th term.

   a 1, 6, 11, 16 …

   b 20, 14, 8, 2 …

   c 2, 5, 8, 11 …

2 Which of the following numbers are irrational?

$$1\frac{5}{8}, \ 0.213231234\ldots, \ \sqrt{25}, \ \frac{7}{17}, \ 0.1, \ -0.654, \ \sqrt{2}, \ \frac{22}{5}, \ 4\pi$$

3 Here is a set of numbers:

$\frac{2}{3}$	$-\frac{3}{5}$	0	−4	25	3.21	$\sqrt{5}$	−2.5	85	0.75

   a Which of these numbers belongs to the set of rational numbers?

   b Which numbers would go into the set $A = \{\text{integers}\}$?

4 $\mathscr{E} = \{x : x \text{ is a whole number between 0 and 11}\}$, 0 and 11 are not elements of $\mathscr{E}$, $A = \{\text{even numbers}\}$ and $B = \{\text{multiples of 3}\}$.

   a Draw a Venn diagram to show the relationships between the sets.

   b List the members of the set $A \cap B$.

   c Determine $n(A \cup B)$.

5 An engineering firm produces metal components for cars. A sample of 120 components was quality tested and it was found that 8 had cracks and 11 were not the right size. 3 components were both cracked and the incorrect size. Determine the number of components that had:

   a one fault only   b no faults

   c at least one fault.

10 Straight lines and quadratic equations

10.1 Straight lines

- The position of a point can be uniquely described on the Cartesian plane using ordered pairs (x, y) of coordinates.
- You can use equations in terms of x and y to generate a table of paired values for x and y. You can plot these on the Cartesian plane and join them to draw a graph. To find y-values in a table of values, substitute the given (or chosen) x-values into the equation and solve for y.
- The gradient of a line describes its slope or steepness. Gradient can be defined as:

$$m = \frac{\text{change in } y}{\text{change in } x}$$

  - lines that slope up to the right have a positive gradient
  - lines that slope down to the right have a negative gradient
  - lines parallel to the x-axis (horizontal lines) have a gradient of 0
  - lines parallel to the y-axis (vertical lines) have an undefined gradient
  - lines parallel to each other have the same gradients.

- The equation of a straight line can be written in general terms as $y = mx + c$, where x and y are coordinates of points on the line, m is the gradient of the line and c is the y-intercept (the point where the graph crosses the y-axis).
- To find the equation of a given line you need to find the y-intercept and substitute this for c. Then you need to find the gradient of the line and substitute this for m.

> ### Tip
> Normally the x-values will be given. If not, choose three small values (for example, −2, 0 and 2). You need a minimum of three points to draw a graph. All graphs should be clearly labelled with their equation.

> Remember, parallel lines have the same gradient.

Exercise 10.1

1 For x-values of −1, 0, 1, 2 and 3, draw a table of values for each of the following equations.

   a $y = x + 5$ **b** $y = -2x - 1$ **c** $y = 7 - 2x$ **d** $y = -x - 2$

   e $x = 4$ **f** $y = -2$ **g** $y = -2x - \frac{1}{2}$ **h** $4 = 2x - 5y$

   i $0 = x - 2y - 1$ **j** $x + y = -\frac{1}{2}$

2 Draw and label graphs (**a**) to (**e**) in question 1 on one set of axes and graphs (**f**) to (**j**) on another.

3 Find the equation of a line parallel to graph (**a**) in question 1 and passing through point $(0, -2)$.

4 Are the following pairs of lines parallel or not?

   a $y = 3x + 3$ and $y = x + 3$ **b** $y = \frac{1}{2}x - 4$ and $y = \frac{1}{2}x - 8$

   c $y = -3x$ and $y = -3x + 7$ **d** $y = 0.8x - 7$ and $y = 8x + 2$

   e $2y = -3x + 2$ and $y = \frac{3}{2}x + 2$ **f** $2y - 3x = 2$ and $y = -1.5x + 2$

   g $y = 8$ and $y = -9$ **h** $x = -3$ and $x = \frac{1}{2}$

5 Find the gradient of the following lines.

a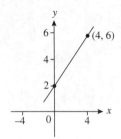

b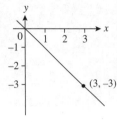

c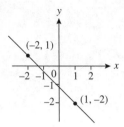

d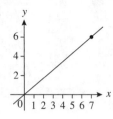

e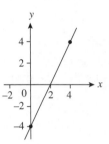

f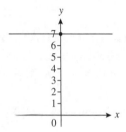

g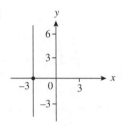

h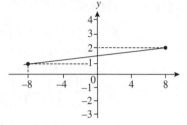

> **Tip**
>
> You may need to rewrite the equations in the form $y = mx + c$ before you can do this.

6 Determine the gradient (m) and the y-intercept (c) of each of the following graphs.

a $y = 3x - 4$

b $y = -x - 1$

c $y = -\frac{1}{2}x + 5$

d $y = x$

e $y = \frac{x}{2} + \frac{1}{4}$

f $y = \frac{4x}{5} - 2$

g $y = 7$

h $y = -3x$

i $x + 3y = 14$

j $x + y + 4 = 0$

k $x - 4 = y$

l $2x = 5 - y$

m $x + \frac{y}{2} = -10$

7 Determine the equation of each of the following graphs.

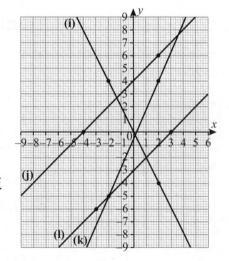

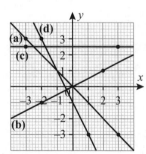

10.2 Quadratic expressions

- A quadratic expression has terms where the highest power of the variable is two (for example x^2).
- You can expand (multiply out) the product of two brackets by multiplying each term of the first bracket by each term of the second. You may then need to add or subtract any like terms.

! **Tip**

The acronym, FOIL, may help you to systematically expand pairs of brackets:

F – first × first

O – outer × outer

I – inner × inner

L – last × last

Exercise 10.2

1 Expand and simplify.

a $(x+2)(x+3)$ **b** $(x+2)(x-3)$

c $(x+5)(x+7)$ **d** $(x-5)(x+7)$

e $(x-1)(x-3)$ **f** $(2x-1)(x+1)$

g $(y-7)(y-2)$ **h** $(2x-y)(3x-2y)$

i $(x^2+1)(2x^2-3)$ **j** $(x-11)(x+12)$

k $\left(\frac{1}{2}x+1\right)\left(1-\frac{1}{2}x\right)$ **l** $(x-3)(2-3x)$

m $(3x-2)(2-4x)$

2 Expand and simplify.

a $(x+4)^2$ **b** $(x-3)^2$ **c** $(x+5)^2$

d $(y-2)^2$ **e** $(x+y)^2$ **f** $(2x-y)^2$

Drawing a diagram will help to make this problem clearer.

3 A carpet fitter has a square of carpet with sides x metres long. To fit the room he needs to cut a 40 cm wide strip off the edge of the square piece and place it along the adjacent side of the square forming a rectangle. Any carpet not needed will be discarded.

a Express the length and breadth of the rectangular carpet in terms of x.

b Write an expression for the area of the rectangular piece.

c What area of carpet is discarded?

Mixed exercise

1 For each equation, copy and complete the table of values. Draw the graphs for all four equations on the same set of axes.

a $y=\frac{1}{2}x$

x	−1	0	2	3
y				

b $y=-\frac{1}{2}x+3$

x	−1	0	2	3
y				

c $y = 2$

x	−1	0	2	3
y				

d $y - 2x - 4 = 0$

x	−1	0	2	3
y				

2 Determine the gradient and the y-intercept of each graph.

   a $y = -2x - 1$ **b** $y + 6 = x$ **c** $x - y = -8$

   d $y = -\frac{1}{2}$ **e** $2x + 3y = 6$ **f** $y = -x$

3 What equation defines each of these lines?

   a a line with a gradient of 1 and a y-intercept of −3

   b a line with a y-intercept of $\frac{1}{2}$ and a gradient of $-\frac{2}{3}$

   c a line parallel to $y = -x + 8$ with a y-intercept of −2

   d a line parallel to $y = -\frac{4}{5}x$ which passes through the point $(0, -3)$

   e a line parallel to $2y - 4x + 2 = 0$ with a y-intercept of −3

   f a line parallel to $x + y = 5$ which passes through $(1, 1)$

   g a line parallel to the x-axis which passes through $(1, 2)$

   h a line parallel to the y-axis which passes through $(-4, -5)$

4 Find the gradient of the following lines.

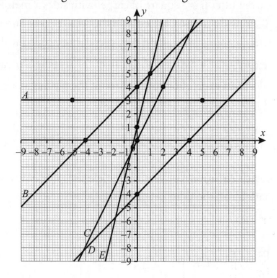

5 What is the equation of each of these lines?

a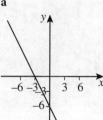

b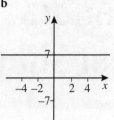

c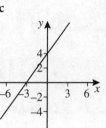

d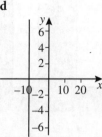

e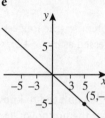

f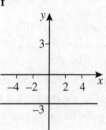

> **Tip**
>
> Time is usually plotted on the horizontal or x-axis because it is the independent variable in most relationships. In this graph you will only need to work in the first quadrant. You won't have any negative values because Caroline cannot run for less than 0 hours and her speed cannot be less than 0 km per hour.

6 Caroline likes running. She averages a speed of 7 km/h when she runs. This relationship can be expressed as $D = 7t$, where D is the distance covered and t is the time (in hours) that she runs for.

a Use the formula $D = 7t$ to draw up a table of values for 0, 2, 4 and 6 hours of running.

b On a set of axes, draw a graph to show the relationship between D and t. Think carefully about how you will number the axes before you start.

c Write an equation in the form of $y = mx + c$ to describe this graph.

d What is the gradient of the line?

e Use your graph to find the time it takes Caroline to run:

  i 21 km   **ii** 10 km   **iii** 5 km.

f Use your graph to find out how far she runs in:

  i 3 hours   **ii** $2\frac{1}{2}$ hours   **iii** $\frac{3}{4}$ of an hour.

g Caroline enters the Two Oceans Marathon. The route is 42 km long, but it is very hilly. She estimates her average speed will drop to around 6 km/h. How long will it take her to complete the race if she runs at 6 km/h?

7 Expand and simplify.

a $(x + 12)(x - 2)$

b $(x - 8)(x + 5)$

c $(2x + 5)(2x + 4)$

d $(2x + 3)^2$

8 Work out the missing values in each equation.

a $(x + 6)(x + 8) = x^2 + \Box x + \Box$

b $(x + \Box)(x + 6) = x^2 + 10x + \Box$

c $(\Box x + \Box)(2x + 7) = 4x^2 + 18x + \Box$

11 Pythagoras' theorem and similar shapes

11.1 Pythagoras' theorem

- In a right-angled triangle, the square of the length of the hypotenuse (the longest side) is equal to the sum of the squares of the lengths of the other two sides. This can be expressed as $c^2 = a^2 + b^2$, where c is the hypotenuse and a and b are the two shorter sides of the triangle.
- Conversely, If $c^2 = a^2 + b^2$ then the triangle will be right-angled.
- To find the length of an unknown side in a right-angled triangle you need to know two of the sides. Then you can substitute the two known lengths into the formula and solve for the unknown length.

Exercise 11.1 A

Tip
The *hypotenuse* is the longest side. It is always opposite the right angle.

1 Calculate the length of the unknown side in each of these triangles.

a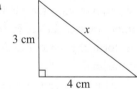

b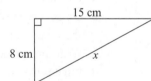

c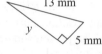

d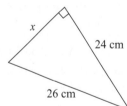

e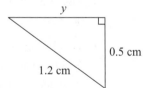

f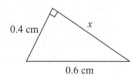

g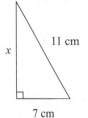

h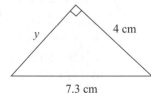

> **! Tip**
> If you get an answer that is an irrational number, round your answer to three significant figures unless the instruction tells you otherwise.

2 Find the length of the side marked with a letter in each figure.

a

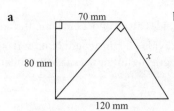

b

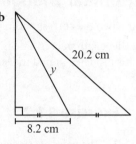

c

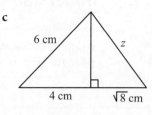

d

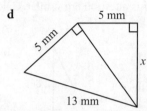

e

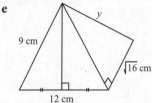

f

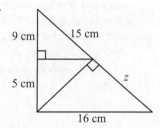

3 Determine whether each of the following triangles is right-angled. Side lengths are all in centimetres.

a

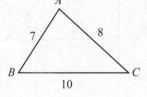

b

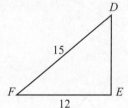

c

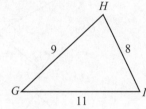

d

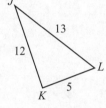

Exercise 11.1 B

> With worded problems, do a rough sketch of the situation, fill in the known lengths and mark the unknown lengths with letters.

1 A rectangle has sides of 12 mm and 16 mm. Calculate the length of one of the diagonals.

2 The size of a rectangular computer screen is determined by the length of the diagonal. Nick buys a 55 cm screen that is 33 cm high. How long is the base of the screen?

3 The sides of an equilateral triangle are 100 mm long. Calculate the perpendicular height of the triangle and hence find its area.

4 A vertical pole is 12 m long. It is supported by two wire stays. The stays are attached to the top of the pole and fixed to the ground. One stay is fixed to the ground 5 m from the base of the pole and the other is fixed to the ground 9 m from the base of the pole. Calculate the length of each wire stay.

5 Nick has a 2.5 m ladder that he uses to reach shelves fixed to the wall of his garage. He wants to reach a shelf that is 2.4 metres above the ground. What is the furthest distance he can place the foot of his ladder from the wall?

11.2 Understanding similar triangles

- Triangles are similar when the corresponding sides are proportional and the corresponding angles are equal in size.
- In similar figures, if the length of each side is divided by the length of its corresponding side, all the answers will be same. You can use this property to find the lengths of unknown sides in similar figures.

> **Tip**
>
> Work out which sides are corresponding before you start. It is helpful to mark corresponding sides in the same colour or with a symbol.

Exercise 11.2

1 The pairs of triangles in this question are similar. Calculate the unknown (lettered) length in each case.

a

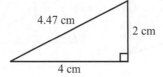

b

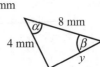

c

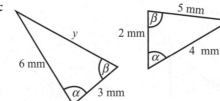

d

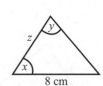

e

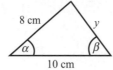

f

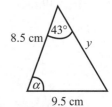

g

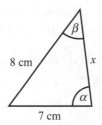

h

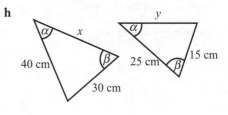

2 Explain fully why triangle *ABC* is similar to triangle *ADE*.

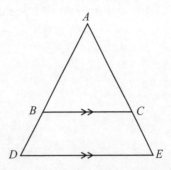

3 Nancy is lying on a blanket on the ground, 4 m away from a 3 m tall tree. When she looks up past the tree she can see the roof of a building which is 30 m beyond the tree. Work out the height of the building.

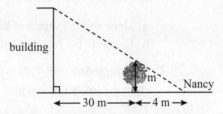

11.3 Understanding congruence

● Congruent shapes are identical in shape and size. Two shapes are congruent if the corresponding sides are equal in length and the corresponding angles are equal in size. Reflections are also congruent.

Exercise 11.3

1 Identify all the shapes that are congruent to *A*.

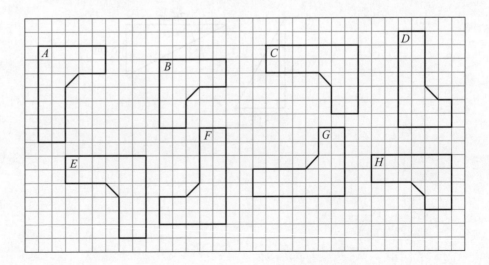

2 Use squared or dotted paper to investigate how many triangles, congruent to this one you can draw on a 3 × 3 grid.

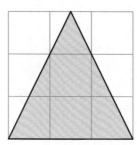

Mixed exercise

1 A school caretaker wants to mark out a sports field 50 m wide and 120 m long. To make sure that the field is rectangular, he needs to know how long each diagonal should be.

   a Draw a rough sketch of the field.
   b Calculate the required lengths of the diagonals.

2 In triangle ABC, $AB = 10$ cm, $BC = 8$ cm and $AC = 6$ cm. Determine whether the triangle is right-angled or not and give reasons for your answer.

3 A triangle with sides of 25 mm, 65 mm and 60 mm is similar to another triangle with its longest side 975 mm. Calculate the perimeter of the larger triangle.

4 Calculate the missing dimensions in each of these pairs of similar triangles.

a
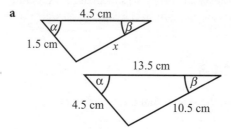

b
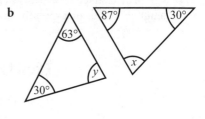

c
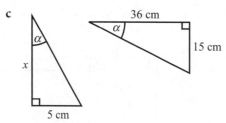

5 Which triangles are congruent in this set?

a   b 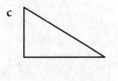   c 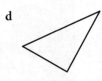   d

6 An 8.6 m long wire cable is used to secure a mast of height x m. The cable is attached to the top of the mast and secured on the ground 6.5 m away from the base of the mast. How tall is the mast? Give your answer correct to two decimal places.

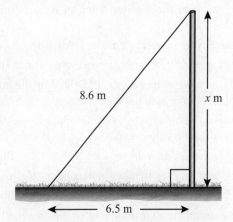

7 Nadia wants to have a metal number 1 made for her gate. She has found a sample brass numeral and noted its dimensions. She decides that her numeral should be similar to this one, but that it should be four times larger.

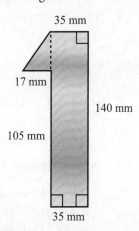

a Draw a rough sketch of the numeral that Nadia wants to make with the correct dimensions written on it in millimetres.
b Calculate the length of the sloping edge at the top of the full size numeral to the nearest whole millimetre.

12 Averages and measures of spread

12.1 Different types of average

- Statistical data can be summarised using an average (measure of central tendency) and a measure of spread (dispersion).
- There are three types of average: mean, median and mode.
- A measure of spread is the range (largest value minus smallest value).
- The mean is the sum of the data items divided by the number of items in the data set. The mean does not have to be one of the numbers in the data set.
  - The mean can be affected by extreme values in the data set. When one value is much lower or higher than the rest of the data it is called an outlier. Outliers skew the mean and make it less representative of the data set.
- The median is the middle value in a set of data when the data is arranged in increasing order.
  - When there is an even number of data items, the median is the mean of the two middle values.
- The mode is the number (or item) that appears most often in a data set.
  - When two numbers appear most often the data has two modes and is said to be bimodal. When more than two numbers appear equally often the mode has no real value as a statistic.

Exercise 12.1

1 Determine the mean, median and mode of the following sets of data.

    a 5, 9, 6, 4, 7, 6, 6
    b 23, 38, 15, 27, 18, 38, 21, 40, 27
    c 12, 13, 14, 12, 12, 13, 15, 16, 14, 13, 12, 11
    d 4, 4, 4, 5, 5, 5, 6, 6, 6
    e 4, 4, 4, 4, 5, 5, 6, 6, 6
    f 4, 4, 5, 5, 5, 6, 6, 6, 6

2 Five students scored a mean mark of 14.8 out of 20 for a maths test.

    a Which of these sets of marks fit this average?
        i   14, 16, 17, 15, 17   **ii** 12, 13, 12, 19, 19   **iii** 12, 19, 12, 18, 13
        iv 13, 17, 15, 16, 17   **v** 19, 19, 12, 0, 19   **vi** 15, 15, 15, 15, 14
    b Compare the sets of numbers in your answer above. Explain why you can get the same mean from different sets of numbers.

3 The mean of 15 numbers is 17. What is the sum of the numbers?

4 The sum of 21 numbers is 312.8. Which of the following numbers is closest to the mean of the 21 numbers? 14, 15, 16 or 17.

Tip

If you multiply the mean by the number of items in the data set, you get the total of the scores. This will help you solve problems like question 2.

5 An agricultural worker wants to know which of two dairy farmers have the best milk producing cows. Farmer Singh says his cows produce 2490 litres of milk per day. Farmer Naidoo says her cows produce 1890 litres of milk per day.
There is not enough information to decide which cows are the better producers of milk. What other information would you need to answer the question?

Siblings are brothers and sisters.

! **Tip**
It may help to draw up a rough frequency table to solve problems like this one.

6 In a group of students, six had four siblings, seven had five siblings, eight had three siblings, nine had two siblings and ten had one sibling.

 a What is the total number students?
 b What is the total number of siblings?
 c What is the mean number of siblings?
 d What is the modal number of siblings?

7 The management of a factory announced salary increases and said that workers would receive an average increase of $20 to $40.
The table shows the old and new salaries of the workers in the factory.

	Previous salary	Salary with increase
Four workers in Category A	$180	$240
Two workers in Category B	$170	$200
Six workers in Category C	$160	$170
Eight workers in Category D	$150	$156

 a Calculate the mean increase for all workers.
 b Calculate the modal increase.
 c What is the median increase?
 d How many workers received an increase of between $20 and $40?
 e Was the management announcement true? Say why or why not.

8 This stem-and-leaf diagram shows the number of texts messages that Mario received on his phone each day for a month.

Number of text messages

Stem	Leaf
2	3 5 5 6 6 6 7
3	2 4 4 6 8 8 8 8 9 9
4	0 1 2 4 4 4 5 7 8 8
5	0 1 5

Key: 2 | 3 = 23 messages

 a What is the range of the data?
 b What is the mode?
 c Determine the median number of messages received.

12.2 Making comparisons using averages and ranges

- You can use averages to compare two or more sets of data. However, averages on their own may be misleading, so it is useful to work with other summary statistics as well.
- The range is a measure of how spread out (dispersed) the data is. Range = largest value – smallest value.
- A large range means that the data is spread out, so the measures of central tendency (averages) may not be representative of the whole data set.

> **Tip**
> When the mean is affected by extreme values the median is more representative of the data.

> **Tip**
> The mode only tells you the most popular value and this is not necessarily representative of the whole data set.

Exercise 12.2

1 For the following sets of data, one of the three averages is not representative. State which one is not representative in each case.

   a 6, 2, 5, 1, 5, 7, 2, 3, 8
   b 2, 0, 1, 3, 1, 6, 2, 9, 10, 3, 2, 2, 0
   c 21, 29, 30, 14, 5, 16, 3, 24, 17

2 Twenty students scored the following results in a test (out of 20).

17	18	17	14	8	3	15	18	3	15
0	17	16	17	14	7	18	19	5	15

   a Calculate the mean, median, mode and range of the marks.
   b Why is the median the best summary statistic for this particular set of data?

3 The table shows the times (in minutes and seconds) that two runners achieved over 800 m during one season.

Runner A	2 m 2.5 s	2 m 1.7 s	2 m 2.2 s	2 m 3.7 s	2 m 1.7 s	2 m 2.9 s	2 m 2.6 s
Runner B	2 m 2.4 s	2 m 1.8 s	2 m 2.3 s	2 m 4.4 s	2 m 0.6 s	2 m 2.2 s	2 m 1.2 s

   a Which runner is the better of the two? Why?
   b Which runner is most consistent? Why?

12.3 Calculating averages and ranges for frequency data

- The mean can be calculated from a frequency table. To calculate the mean you add a column to the table and calculate the score × frequency (*fx*). Mean = $\dfrac{\text{total of (score} \times \text{frequency) column}}{\text{total of frequency column}}$.
- Find the mode in a table by looking at the frequency column. The data item with the highest frequency is the mode.
- In a frequency table, the data is already ordered by size. To find the median, work out its position in the data and then add the frequencies till you equal or exceed this value. The score in this category will be the median.

Exercise 12.3

Score	Frequency
0	
1	
2	
3	
4	
5	
6	

1 Copy and complete the frequency table for the data below and then calculate:

   a the mean   **b** the mode   **c** the median   **d** the range.

0	3	4	3	3	2	2	2	2	1
3	3	4	3	6	2	2	2	0	0
5	4	3	2	4	3	3	3	2	1
3	1	1	1	1	0	0	0	2	4

2 For each of the following frequency distributions calculate:

   a the mean score   **b** the median score   **c** the modal score.

Data set A

Score	1	2	3	4	5	6
Frequency	12	14	15	12	15	12

Data set B

Score	10	20	30	40	50	60	70	80
Frequency	13	25	22	31	16	23	27	19

Data set C

Score	1.5	2.5	3.5	4.5	5.5	6.5
Frequency	15	12	15	12	10	21

Mixed exercise

1 Find the mean, median, mode and range of the following sets of data.

a 6	5	6	7	4	5	8	6	7	10
b 6	3	2	4	2	1	2	2	1	
c 12.5	13.2	19.4	12.8	7.5	18.6	12.6			

2 The mean of two consecutive numbers is 9.5. The mean of eight different numbers is 4.7.

   a Calculate the total of the first two numbers.

   b What are these two numbers?

   c Calculate the mean of the ten numbers together.

3 Three suppliers sell specialised remote controllers for access systems. A sample of 100 remote controllers is taken from each supplier and the working life of each controller is measured in weeks. The following table shows the mean time and range for each supplier.

Supplier	Mean (weeks)	Range (weeks)
A	137	16
B	145	39
C	141	16

Which supplier would you recommend to someone who is looking to buy a remote controller? Why?

4 A box contains 50 plastic blocks of different volume as shown in the frequency table.

Volume (cm³)	2	3	4	5	6	7
Frequency	4	7	9	12	10	8

   a Find the mean volume of the blocks.

   b What volume is most common?

   c What is the median volume?

13 Understanding measurement

13.1 Understanding units

- Units of measure in the metric system are metres (m), grams (g) and litres (l). Sub-divisions have prefixes such as milli- and centi-; the prefix kilo is a multiple.
- To convert from a larger unit to a smaller unit you multiply the measurement by the correct multiple of ten.
- To convert from a smaller unit to a larger unit you divide the measurement by the correct multiple of ten.

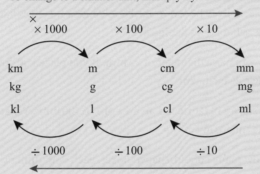

- Area is always measured in square units. To convert areas from one unit to another you need to square the appropriate length conversion factor.
- Volume is measured in cubic units. To convert volumes from one unit to another you need to cube the appropriate length conversion factor.

Exercise 13.1

Tip

Memorise these conversions:

10 mm = 1 cm

100 cm = 1 m

1000 m = 1 km

1000 mg = 1 g

1000 g = 1 kg

1000 kg = 1 t

1000 ml = 1 litre

1 cm³ = 1 ml

1 Use the conversion diagram in the box above as a basis to draw your own diagrams to show how to convert:

  a units of area   **b** units of volume.

2 Convert the following length measurements to the units given:

  a 2.6 km = _____ m   **b** 23 cm = _____ mm

  c 8.2 m = _____ cm   **d** 2 450 809 m = _____ km

  e 0.02 m = _____ mm   **f** 15.7 cm = _____ m.

3 Convert the following measurements of mass to the units given:

  a 9.08 kg = _____ g   **b** 49.34 kg = _____ g

  c 0.5 kg = _____ g   **d** 68 g = _____ kg

  e 15.2 g = _____ kg   **f** 2 300 000 g = _____ tonne.

4 Identify the greater length in each of these pairs of lengths. Then calculate the difference between the two lengths. Give your answer in the most appropriate units.

a	19 km	18 900 m	**b**	90 m	9015 cm
c	43.3 cm	435 mm	**d**	492 cm	4.29 m
e	635 m	0.6 km	**f**	5.8 km	580 500 cm

5 Convert the following area measurements to the units given:

a $12\,cm^2 = $ _____ mm^2 **b** $9\,cm^2 = $ _____ mm^2

c $164.2\,cm^2 = $ _____ mm^2 **d** $0.37\,km^2 = $ _____ m^2

e $9441\,m^2 = $ _____ km^2 **f** $0.423\,m^2 = $ _____ mm^2.

6 Convert the following volume measurements to the units given:

a $69\,cm^3 = $ _____ mm^3 **b** $19\,cm^3 = $ _____ mm^3

c $30.04\,cm^3 = $ _____ mm^3 **d** $4.815\,m^3 = $ _____ cm^3

e $103\,mm^3 = $ _____ cm^3 **f** $46\,900\,mm^3 = $ _____ m^3.

7 Naeem lives 1.2 km from school and Sadiqa lives 980 m from school. How much closer to the school does Sadiqa live?

8 A coin has a diameter of 22 mm. If you placed 50 coins in a row, how long would the row be in cm?

9 A square of fabric has an area of 176 400 mm². What are the lengths of the sides of the square in cm?

10 How many cuboid-shaped boxes, each with dimensions 50 cm × 90 cm × 120 cm, can you fit into a volume of 48 m³?

Cubic centimetres or cm³ is sometimes written as cc. For example, a scooter may have a 50 cc engine. That means the total volume of all cylinders in the engine is 50 cm³.

13.2 Time

- Time is not decimal. 1 h 15 means one hour and $\frac{15}{60}$ (or $\frac{1}{4}$) of an hour, not 1.15 h.
- One hour and 15 minutes is written as 1:15.
- Time can be written using a.m. and p.m. notation or as a 24-hour time using the numbers from 0 to 24 to give the times from 12 midnight on one day (00:00 h) to one second before midnight (23:59:59). Even in the 24-hour clock system, time is not decimal. The time one minute after 15:59 is 16:00.

Tip

You can express parts of an hour as a decimal. Divide the number of minutes by 60.

For example 12 minutes $= \frac{12}{60} = \frac{1}{5} = 0.2$ hours. This can make your calculations easier.

Exercise 13.2

1 Five people record the time they start work, the time they finish and the length of their lunch break.

a Copy and complete this table to show how much time each person spent at work on this particular day.

Name	Time in	Time out	Lunch	Hours worked
Dawoot	$\frac{1}{4}$ past 9	Half past five	$\frac{3}{4}$ hour	
Nadira	8:17 a.m.	5:30 p.m.	$\frac{1}{2}$ hour	
John	08:23	17:50	45 min	
Robyn	7:22 a.m.	4:30 p.m.	1 hour	
Mari	08:08	18:30	45 min	

b Calculate each person's daily earnings to the nearest whole cent if they are paid $7.45 per hour.

2 On a particular day, the low tide in Hong Kong harbour is at 09:15. The high tide is at 15:40 the same day. How much time passes between low tide and high tide?

3 Sarah's plane was due to land at 2:45 p.m. However, it was delayed and it landed at 15:05. How much later did the plane arrive than it was meant to?

4 How much time passes between:

a 2:25 p.m. and 8:12 p.m. on the same day?
b 1:43 a.m. and 12:09 p.m. on the same day?
c 6:33 p.m. and 6:45 a.m. the next day?
d 1:09 a.m. and 15:39 on the same day?

5 Use this section from a bus timetable to answer the questions that follow.

Chavez Street	09:00	09:30	10:00
Castro Avenue	09:18	09:48	10:18
Peron Place	09:35	10:05	10:35
Marquez Lane	10:00	10:30	11:00

a What is the earliest bus from Chavez Street?
b How long does the journey from Chavez Street to Marquez Lane take?
c A bus arrives at Peron Place at quarter past ten. The bus is 10 minutes late. At what time did it leave Chavez Street?
d Sanchez misses the 09:48 bus from Castro Avenue. How long will have to wait before the next scheduled bus arrives?
e The 10:00 bus from Chavez Street is delayed in roadworks between Castro Avenue and Peron Place for 19 minutes. How will this affect the rest of the timetable?

13.3 Upper and lower bounds

- All measurements we make are rounded to some degree of accuracy. The degree of accuracy (for example the nearest metre or to two decimal places) allows you to work out the highest and lowest possible value of the measurements. The highest possible value is called the upper bound and the lowest possible value is called the lower bound.

dp means decimal places
sf means significant figures

Exercise 13.3

1 Each of the numbers below has been rounded to the degree of accuracy shown in the brackets. Find the upper and lower bounds in each case.

    a 42 (nearest whole number)
    b 13 325 (nearest whole number)
    c 400 (1sf)
    d 12.24 (2dp)
    e 11.49 (2dp)
    f 2.5 (to nearest tenth)
    g 390 (nearest ten)
    h 1.132 (4sf)

2 A building is 72 m tall measured to the nearest metre.

    a What are the upper and lower bounds of the building's height?
    b Is 72.499999999999999999 metres a possible height for the building? Explain why or why not.

13.4 Conversion graphs

- Conversion graphs allow you to convert from one unit of measure to another by providing the values of both units on different axes. To find one value (x) when the other (y) is given, you need to find the y-value against the graph and then read off the corresponding value on the other axis.

Exercise 13.4

Tip
Make sure you read the labels on the axis so that you are reading off the correct values.

1 Sheila, an Australian, is going on holiday to the island of Bali in Indonesia. She finds this conversion graph to show the value of rupiah (the currency of Indonesia) against the Australian dollar.

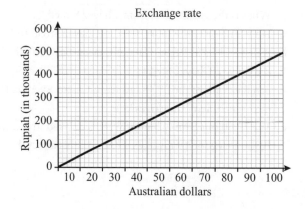

a   What is the scale on the vertical axis?

b   How many rupiah will Sheila get for:

   i   Aus $50   ii   Aus $100   iii   Aus $500?

c   The hotel she plans to stay at charges 400 000 rupiah a night.

   i   What is this amount in Australian dollars?

   ii   How much will Sheila pay in Australian dollars for an eight night stay?

2   Study the conversion graph and answer the questions.

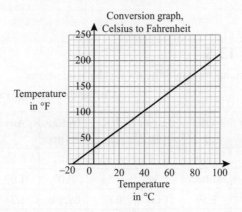

a   What is shown on the graph?

b   What is the temperature in Fahrenheit when it is:

   i   0 °C   ii   10 °C   iii   100 °C?

c   Sarah finds a recipe for chocolate brownies that says she needs to cook the mixture at 210 °C for one hour. After an hour she finds that it has hardly cooked at all. What could the problem be?

d   Jess is American. When she calls her friend Nick in England she says, 'It's really cold here, must be about 50 degrees out.' What temperature scale is she using? How do you know this?

3   This graph shows the conversion factor for pounds (Imperial measurement of mass) and kilograms.

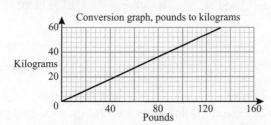

a   Nettie says she needs to lose about 20 pounds. How much is this in kilograms?

b   John says he's a weakling. He weighs 98 pounds. How much does he weigh in kilograms?

c   Which is the greater mass in each of these cases:

   i   30 pounds or 20 kilograms

   ii   35 kilograms or 70 pounds

   iii   60 kilograms or 145 pounds?

> **! Tip**
>
> The USA mainly still uses the Fahrenheit scale for temperature. Appliances, such as stoves, may have temperatures in Fahrenheit on them, particularly if they are an American brand.

13.5 More money

- When you change money from one currency to another you do so at a given rate of exchange. Changing to another currency is called buying foreign currency.
- Exchange rates can be worked out using conversion graphs (as in 13.4), but more often, they are worked out by doing calculations.
- Doing calculations with money is just like doing calculations with decimals but you need to remember to include the currency symbols in your answers.

Exercise 13.5

Use the exchange rate table below for these questions.

Currency exchange rates

Currency	US $	Euro (€)	UK £	Indian Rupee	Aus $	Can $	SA Rand	NZ $	Yen (¥)
1 US $	1.00	0.72	0.63	49.81	0.97	1.01	9.08	1.25	76.16
inverse	1.00	1.39	1.59	0.02	1.03	0.99	0.12	0.80	0.01
1 Euro	1.39	1.00	0.87	69.10	1.34	1.40	11.21	1.73	105.64
inverse	0.72	1.00	1.15	0.01	0.74	0.71	0.09	0.58	0.01
1 UK £	1.59	1.15	1.00	79.37	1.54	1.61	12.88	1.99	121.36
inverse	0.63	0.87	1.00	0.01	0.65	0.62	0.08	0.50	0.01

> **Tip**
> Currency rates change all the time. You need to read tables carefully and use the rates that are given.

> The inverse rows show the exchange rate of one unit of the currency in the column to the currency above the word inverse. For example, using the inverse row below US $ and the euro column, €1 will buy $1.39.

a What is the exchange rate for:
- **i** US$ to yen
- **ii** UK£ to NZ$
- **iii** Euro to Indian rupee
- **iv** Canadian dollar to euro
- **v** Yen to pound
- **vi** South African rand to US$?

b How many Indian rupees will you get for:
- **i** US$50
- **ii** 600 euros
- **iii** £95?

c How many yen will you need to buy:
- **i** US$120
- **ii** 500 euros
- **iii** £1200?

Mixed exercise

1 Convert the following measurements to the units given.

- **a** 2.7 km to metres
- **b** 69 cm to mm
- **c** 6 tonnes to kilograms
- **d** 23.5 grams to kilograms
- **e** 263 grams to milligrams
- **f** 29.25 litres to millilitres
- **g** 240 ml to litres
- **h** $10\,cm^2$ to mm^2
- **i** $6428\,m^2$ to km^2
- **j** $7.9\,m^3$ to cm^3
- **k** $0.029\,km^3$ to m^3
- **l** $168\,mm^3$ to cm^3

2 The average time taken to walk around a track is one minute and 35 seconds. How long will it take you to walk around the track 15 times at this rate?

3 A journey took 3 h 40 min and 10 s to complete. Of this, 1 h 20 min and 15 s was spent having lunch or stops for other reasons. The rest of the time was spent travelling. How much time was actually spent travelling?

4 Tayo's height is 1.62 m, correct to the nearest cm. Calculate the least possible and greatest possible height that he could be.

5 The number of people who attended a meeting was given as 50, correct to the nearest 10.

    a Is it possible that 44 people attended? Explain why or why not?

    b Is it possible that 54 people attended? Explain why or why not?

6 Study the graph and answer the questions.

> The US gallon is different from the imperial gallon with a conversion factor of 1 US gallon to 3.785 litres.

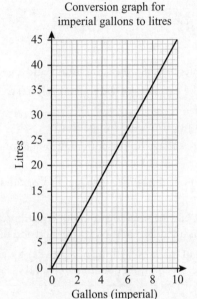

Conversion graph for imperial gallons to litres

    a What does the graph show?

    b Convert to litres:

        i 10 gallons   **ii** 25 gallons

    c Convert to gallons:

        i 15 litres   **ii** 120 litres

    d Naresh says he gets 30 mpg in the city and 42 mpg on the highway in his car.

        i Convert each rate to km per gallon.

        ii Given that one gallon is equivalent to 4.546 litres, convert both rates to kilometres per litre.

> 1 mile = 1.61 km

Use the exchange rate table on page 80 to answer the following questions.

7 Jan lives in South Africa and is going on holiday to Italy. He has R10 000 to exchange for euros. How many euros will he get?

8 Pete is an American who is travelling to India for business. He needs to exchange $2000 for rupees.

    a What is the exchange rate?

    b How many rupees will he get at this rate?

    c At the end of the trip he has 12 450 rupees left over. What will he get if he changes these back to dollars at the given rate?

9 Jimmy is British and he is going to Spain on a package holiday. The cost of the holiday is 4875 euros. What is this amount in UK pounds?

14 Further solving of equations and inequalities

14.1 Simultaneous linear equations

- Simultaneous means 'at the same time'.
- There are two methods for solving simultaneous equations: graphically and algebraically.
- The graphical solution is the point where the two lines of the equations intersect. This point has an x- and a y-coordinate.
- There are two algebraic methods: by substitution and by elimination.
  - Sometimes you need to manipulate or rearrange one or both of the equations before you can solve them algebraically.
  - For the elimination method you need either the same coefficient of x or the same coefficient of y in both equations.
  - If the variable with the same coefficient has the same sign in both equations, you should then subtract one equation from the other. If the signs are different then you should add the two equations.
  - If an equation contains fractions, you can make everything much easier by 'getting rid' of the fractions. Multiply each term by a suitable number (a common denominator) and 'clear' the denominators of the fractions.

Exercise 14.1

1 Draw the graphs for each pair of equation given. Then use the point of intersection to find the simultaneous solution. The limits of the x-axis that you should use are given in each case.

    a $2x + 3 = y$;
       $x - y = 0$; $(-5 < x < 5)$

    b $4x + 2 = y$;
       $x - 2y = 3$; $(-5 < x < 5)$

    c $y = 2x + 2$;
       $2y + 3x - 1 = 0$; $(-5 < x < 10)$

    d $y - x = 4$;
       $y = -x - 7$; $(-10 < x < 5)$

    e $3x + 3y = 3$;
       $y = -2x + 3$; $(-5 < x < 5)$

2 Use the graph below to find:

  a the equations of lines (A) to (F)

  b the solutions to the following pairs of simultaneous equations.

    i (A) and (C)   **ii** (D) and (E)   **iii** (A) and (F)

  c Now check your solutions algebraically.

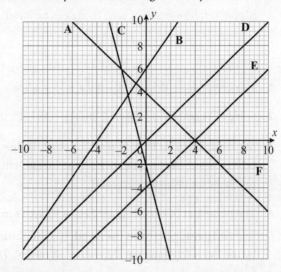

3 Solve for x and y by using the substitution method. Check each solution by substituting the values into one of the equations.

  a $y = 2$ **b** $y - x = 3$ **c** $x + y = 4$ **d** $2x + y = 7$

    $x + y = 6$ $y - 3x = 5$ $2x + 3y = 12$ $3x - y = 8$

4 Solve for x and y by using the elimination method. Check each solution by substituting the values into one of the equations.

  a $x + y = 5$ **b** $3x - y = 1$ **c** $2x + 3y = 12$

    $x - y = 7$ $2x + y = 4$ $3x + 3y = -6$

  d $2x + 3y = 6$ **e** $2x - 5y = 11$ **f** $y - 2x = 1$

    $4x - 6y = -4$ $3x + 2y = 7$ $2y - 3x = 5$

5 Solve simultaneously.

  a $3x + y = 7$ **b** $4x + 2y = 12$ **c** $3x + 2y = 4$

    $3x - y = 5$ $x + 2y = 6$ $2x + y = 3$

  d $2x + 3y = 12$ **e** $5x + 2y = 20$ **f** $3x + 2y = 16$

    $x + 4y = 11$ $x + 4y = 13$ $2x + 3y = 14$

  g $7x - 6y = 17$ **h** $6x + 2y = 2$ **i** $2x - 9y = 0$

    $2x + 3y = 19$ $5x - 7y = 6$ $x - 18y = 27$

6 Sally bought two chocolate bars and one box of gums for $3.15 and Evan paid $2.70 for one chocolate and two boxes of gums. If they bought the same brands and sizes of products, what is the cost of a chocolate bar and the cost of a box of gums?

7 It costs $5 for an adult and $2 for a student to visit the National Botanical Gardens. Adults can be members of the Botanical Society and if you are a member, you can visit the gardens for free. A group of 30 adults and students visited the gardens. Five members of the group could go in for free and it cost the rest of the group $104 to go in. How many students were in the group?

8 Ephrahim has 12 coins in his pocket, consisting of quarters and dimes only. If he has $2.10 in his pocket, how many of each coin does he have?

Mixed exercise

1 Solve for x and y if $3x + y = 1$ and $x - 2y = 12$.

2 Solve for x and y if $3y + 4x = 7$ and $2y + 3x - 4 = 0$.

p.a. stands for 'per annum', which means 'per year'.

3 Mr Habib has $15 000 to invest. His portfolio has two parts, one which yields 5% p.a. and the other 8% p.a. The total interest on the investment was $1050 at the end of the first year. How much did he invest at each rate?

4 The perimeter of a rectangular field is 9 metres in length.

The relationship between the length (L) and the breadth (B) of the rectangle can be expressed by the following equation, $5L - 2B = 12$ metres. Determine the length and the breadth of the field.

5 The graph shows two lines that meet at a point. Use the graph to find:

a the equations of lines

b the solution to the pair of simultaneous equations.

c Now check your solutions algebraically.

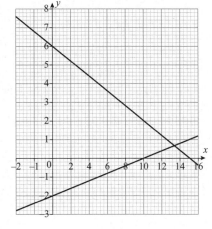

15 Scale drawing, bearings and trigonometry

15.1 Scale drawings

- The scale of a diagram, or a map, can be given as a fraction or a ratio.
- A scale of 1 : 50 000 means that every line in the diagram has a length which is $\frac{1}{50000}$ of the length of the line that it represents in real life. For example 1 cm in the diagram represents 50 000 cm (or 0.5 km) in real life.

Exercise 15.1

REWIND

Revise your metric conversions from chapter 13. ◄

1 a The basic pitch size of a rugby field is 100 m long and 70 m wide. A scale drawing of a field is made with a scale of 1 cm to 10 m. What is the length and width of the field in the drawing?

b The pitch size, including the area inside the goal, is 144 m long and 70 m wide. What are these dimensions in the drawing of this pitch?

2 a The pitch size of a standard hockey field is 91.4 m long and 55 m wide. A scale drawing of a hockey field is made with a scale of 1 : 1000. What are the dimensions of the hockey field in the drawing?

b A school that wants to hold a Seven-A-Side hockey tournament has three standard hockey fields at their Sports Centre. Would it be possible to have five matches taking place at the same time, if the size of the pitch used for Seven-A-Side hockey is 55 m × 43 m?

A5 is half A4 and has dimensions 14.8 cm × 21 cm.

3 a The size of a tennis court is 23.77 m × 10.97 m. What would be a good scale for a drawing of a tennis court if you can only use half of an A4 page? Express this scale as a fraction.

b i Make an accurate scale drawing, using your scale. Include all the markings as shown in the diagram below.

ii The net posts are placed 1 m outside the doubles side lines. Mark each net post with an *x* on your scale drawing.

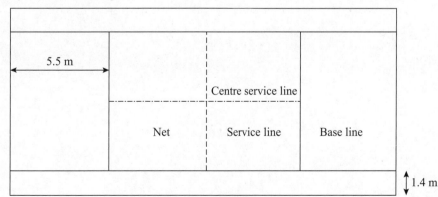

5.5 m

Centre service line

Net   Service line   Base line

Singles side line

1.4 m

Doubles side line

4 a The karate combat area measures 8 m × 8 m. Using a scale drawing and a scale of your choice, calculate the length of the diagonal.

b What would be a more accurate way to determine the length of the diagonal?

15.2 Bearings

- A bearing is a way of describing direction.
- Bearings are measured clockwise from the north direction.
- Bearings are always expressed using three figures.

Exercise 15.2

1 Give the three-figure bearing corresponding to:

a east   b south-west   c north-west.

2 Write down the three-figure bearings of X from Y.

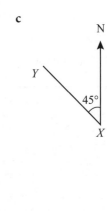

3 Village A is 7.5 km east and 8 km north of village B. Village C is 5 km from village B on a bearing of 300°. Using a scale drawing with a scale of 1 : 100 000 find:

a the bearing of village B from village A
b the bearing of village A from village C
c the direct distance between village B and village A
d the direct distance between village C and village A.

15.3 Understanding the tangent, cosine and sine ratios

- The hypotenuse is the longest side of a right-angled triangle.
- The opposite side is the side opposite a specified angle.
- The adjacent side is the side that forms a specified angle with the hypotenuse.
- The tangent ratio is $\dfrac{\text{the opposite side}}{\text{the adjacent side}}$ of a specified angle.
  - $\tan\theta = \dfrac{\text{opp}(\theta)}{\text{adj}(\theta)}$, $\quad \text{opp}(\theta) = \text{adj}(\theta) \times \tan\theta$, $\quad \text{adj}(\theta) = \dfrac{\text{opp}(\theta)}{\tan\theta}$
- The sine ratio is $\dfrac{\text{the opposite side}}{\text{the hypotenuse}}$ of a specified angle.
  - $\sin\theta = \dfrac{\text{opp}(\theta)}{\text{hyp}}$, $\quad \text{opp}(\theta) = \text{hyp} \times \sin\theta$, $\quad \text{hyp} = \dfrac{\text{opp}(\theta)}{\sin\theta}$
- The cosine ratio is $\dfrac{\text{the adjacent side}}{\text{the hypotenuse}}$ of a specified angle.
  - $\cos\theta = \dfrac{\text{adj}(\theta)}{\text{hyp}}$, $\quad \text{adj}(\theta) = \text{hyp} \times \cos\theta$, $\quad \text{hyp} = \dfrac{\text{adj}(\theta)}{\cos\theta}$

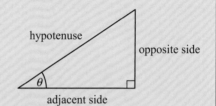

Exercise 15.3

1 Copy and complete the following table:

	a	b	c	d
	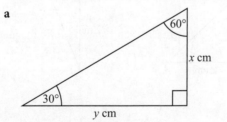			
hypotenuse				
opp(A)				
adj(A)				

Remember, when working with right-angled triangles you may still need to use Pythagoras.

2 Copy and complete the statement(s) alongside each triangle.

a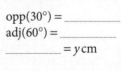

opp(30°) = ...
adj(60°) = ...
.... = y cm

b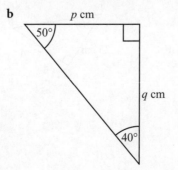

.... (40°) = q cm
.... (50°) = q cm
.... = p cm

3 Calculate the value of the following tangent ratios, using your calculator. Give your answers to two decimal places where necessary.

   a $\tan 33°$ **b** $\tan 55°$ **c** $\tan 79°$

   d $\tan 22.5°$ **e** $\tan 0°$

4 Copy and complete the statements for each of the following triangles, giving your answer as a fraction in its lowest terms where necessary:

   a   **b**   **c**

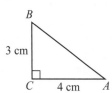 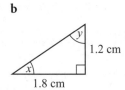 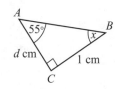

   $\tan A =$ $\tan x =$ $\tan 55° =$

                                    $\tan y =$ $x =$

                                                                   $\tan B =$

   d   **e**

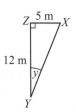 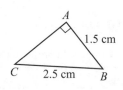

   $\tan y =$ $AC =$

   angle $X =$ $\tan B =$

   $\tan X =$ $\tan C =$

5 Calculate the unknown length (to two decimal places) in each case presented below.

   a   **b**   **c**

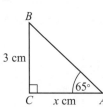 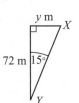 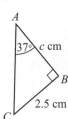

   d   **e**

6 Find, correct to one decimal place, the acute angles that have the following tangent ratios:

   a 0.5   **b** 0.866   **c** 1.25   **d** 12

   e $\frac{1}{4}$ **f** $\frac{13}{15}$ **g** $5\frac{1}{2}$ **h** $\frac{61}{63}$

7 Find, correct to the nearest degree, the value of the lettered angles in the following diagrams.

a
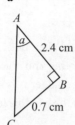

b
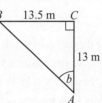

c
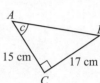

d
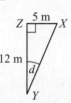

e
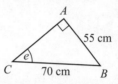

8 For each triangle find:

   i hyp =   **ii** adj(θ) =   **iii** cos θ =

a

b
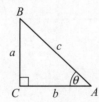

c
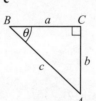

d
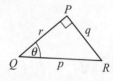

e

9 For each of the following triangles write down the value for:

   i sine   **ii** cosine   **iii** tangent of the marked angle.

a
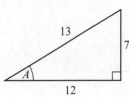

b
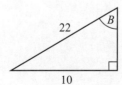

c

d
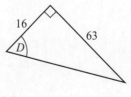

e
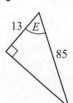

10 Use your calculator to find to the nearest degree:

    a an acute angle whose sine is 0.707

    b an acute angle whose cosine is 0.438

    c an acute angle whose cosine is 0.55

    d an acute angle whose sine is $\dfrac{\sqrt{3}}{2}$

    e an acute angle whose sine is $\dfrac{1}{2}$

    f an acute angle whose tangent is 0.5.

11 The diagram shows two ladders placed in an alley, both reaching up to window ledges on opposite sides: one is twice as long as the other and reaches height H, while the shorter one reaches a height h. The length of the longer ladder is 7.5 m. If the angles of inclination of the ladders are as shown, how much higher is the window ledge of the one window than that of the other?

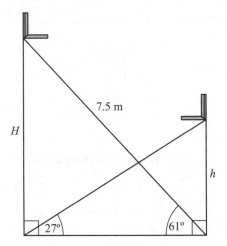

Mixed exercise

1 Find x:

    a $\dfrac{\sin x}{5.2} = \dfrac{\sin 121°}{7.3}$

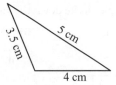

    b

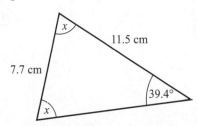

2 A triangle has sides of length 5.7 cm, 7.1 cm and 4.1 cm. If the angle opposite the length of 4.1 cm is 35.3°, what are the other angles?

16 Scatter diagrams and correlation

16.1 Introduction to bivariate data

- When you collect two sets of data in pairs, it is called bivariate data. For example you could collect height and mass data for various students.

- Bivariate data can be plotted on a scatter diagram in order to look for correlation – a relationship between the data. For example, if you wanted to know whether taller students weighed more than smaller students, you could plot the two sets of data (height and mass) on a scatter diagram.

- Correlation is described as positive or negative, and strong or weak. When the points follow no real pattern, there is no correlation.

- A line of best fit can be drawn on a scatter diagram to describe the correlation. This line should follow the direction of the points on the graph and there should be more or less the same number of points on each side of the line. You can use a line of best fit to make predictions within the range of the data shown. It is not statistically accurate to predict beyond the values plotted.

Exercise 16.1

1 Match each graph below to a description of the correlation shown.

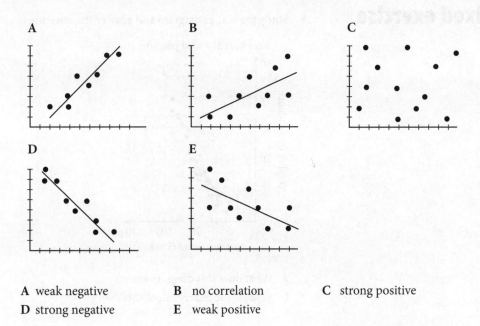

A weak negative   B no correlation   C strong positive
D strong negative   E weak positive

2 Sookie collected data from 15 students in her school athletics team. She wanted to see if there was a correlation between the height of the students and the distance they could jump in the long-jump event. She drew a scatter diagram to show the data.

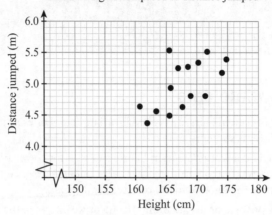

Student heights compared to distance jumped

a Copy the diagram and draw the line of best fit on to it.

b Use your line of best fit to estimate how far a student 165 cm tall could jump.

c For the age group of Sookie's school team, the girls' record for long jump is 6.07 m. How tall would you expect a girl to be who could equal the record jump?

d Describe the correlation shown on the graph.

e What does the correlation indicate about the relationship between height and how far you can jump in the long jump event?

Mixed exercise

1 Study the scatter diagram and answer the questions.

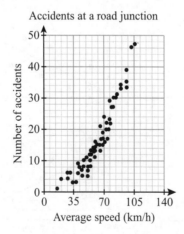

Accidents at a road junction

a What does this diagram show?

b What is the independent variable?

c Copy the diagram and draw a line of best. Use your best fit line to predict:

   i the number accidents at the junction when the average speed of vehicles is 100 km/h

   ii what the average speed of vehicles is when there are fewer than 10 accidents.

d Describe the correlation.

e What does your answer to (**d**) tell you about the relationship between speed and the number of accidents at a junction?

2 A brand new car (Model X) costs $15 000. Mr. Smit wants to find out what price second-hand Model X cars are sold for. He drew this scatter graph to show the relationship between the price and the age of cars in a second-hand car dealership.

Comparison of car age with re-sale price

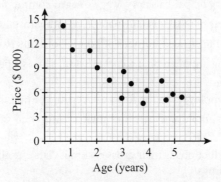

a Describe the trend shown on this graph.

b Between which two years does the price of the car fall in value by the largest amount?

c Describe what happens to the price when the car is 3 to 5 years old.

d How old would you expect a second-hand Model X car to be if it was advertised for sale at $7500?

e What price range would you expect a 3-year-old Model X to fall into?

17 Managing money

17.1 Earning money

- People who are formally employed may be paid a salary, wage or earn commission.
  - A salary is a fixed amount for a year of work, usually paid in monthly instalments.
  - A wage is an agreed hourly rate for an agreed number of hours, normally paid weekly.
  - Workers who sell things for a living are often paid a commission. This is a percentage of the value of the goods sold.
- Additional amounts may be paid to employees in the form of overtime or bonuses.
- Employers may deduct amounts from employees' earnings such as insurance, union dues, medical aid and taxes.
- The amount a person earns before deductions is their gross earnings. The amount they actually are paid after deductions is their net earnings.

Exercise 17.1

Casual workers are normally paid an hourly rate for the hours they work.

> **! Tip**
> Remember, work out all percentage deductions on the gross income and then subtract them all from the gross.

Some workers are paid for each piece of work they complete. This is called piece work.

1 A woman works a 38-hour week. She earns $731.88. What is her hourly rate of pay?

2 What is the annual salary of a person who is paid $2130 per month?

3 An electrician's assistant earns $25.50 per hour for a 35-hour week. He is paid 1.5 times his hourly rate for each hour he works above 35 hours. How much would he earn in a week if he worked:

a 36 hours   **b** 40 hours   **c** 30 hours   **d** $42\frac{1}{2}$ hours?

4 Sandile earns a gross salary of $1613.90 per month. His employer deducts 15% income tax, $144.20 insurance and 1.5% for union dues. What is Sandile's net salary?

5 A clothing factory worker in Indonesia is paid the equivalent of $1.67 per completed garment. How much would he earn if he completed 325 garments in a month?

6 Naadira receives an annual salary of $32 500. She pays 4% of her weekly gross earnings into her pension fund. An additional $93.50 is deducted each week from her salary. Calculate:

a her weekly gross earnings
b her weekly pension fund payment
c her net income per week.

17.2 Borrowing and investing money

- When you borrow money you may pay interest on the amount borrowed.
- When you invest or save money you may earn interest on the amount invested.
- If the amount of interest paid (or charged) is the same for each year, then it is called simple interest.
- When the interest for one year is added to the investment (or debt) and the interest for the next year is calculated on the increased investment (or debt), it is called compound interest.
- The original amount borrowed or invested is called the principal.
- For simple interest, the interest per annum = interest rate × principal (original sum invested).
- The formula used to calculate simple interest is: $I = \dfrac{PRT}{100}$ where:
    - P = the principal
    - R = the interest rate
    - T = the time (in years).
- For compound interest, knowing how to use a multiplier can help you do the calculations faster.
    - For example, if the compound interest is 5%, then the multiplier is $\dfrac{105}{100} = 1.05$.
    - Multiply the principal by a power of the multiplier. The number of years of the investment tells you what the power is. So, if it you invest a sum for three years at 5%, you would multiply by $(1.05)^3$. This gives you the final amount.
- You also need to know the formula for calculating the value (V) of an investment when it is subject to compound interest.
    - $V = P\left(1 + \dfrac{r}{100}\right)^n$, where P is the original amount invested, r is the rate of interest and n is the number of years of compound growth.
- Hire purchase (HP) is a method of buying things on credit and paying them off over an agreed period of time. Normally you pay a deposit and equal monthly instalments.

Exercise 17.2

'per annum' (p.a.) means 'per year'

Tip

You can change the subject of the simple interest formula:

$I = \dfrac{PRT}{100}$

$P = \dfrac{100I}{RT}$

$R = \dfrac{100I}{PT}$

$T = \dfrac{100I}{PR}$

1 Calculate the simple interest on:

   a $250 invested for a year at the rate of 3% per annum
   b $400 invested for five years at the rate of 8% per annum
   c $700 invested for two years at the rate of 15% per annum
   d $800 invested for eight years at the rate of 7% per annum
   e $5000 invested for 15 months at the rate of 5.5% per annum.

2 $7500 is invested at 3.5% per annum simple interest. How long will it take for the amount to reach $8812.50?

3 The total simple interest on $1600 invested for 5 years is $224. What is the percentage rate per annum?

4 The cash price of a car was $20 000. The hire purchase price was a $6000 deposit and instalments of $700 per month for two years. How much more than the cash price was the hire purchase price?

5 Lebo can pay $7999 cash for a new car or he can buy it on HP by paying a $2000 deposit and 36 monthly payments of $230. How much extra will he pay by buying on HP?

6 Calculate the compound interest on:

    a $250 invested for a year at the rate of 3% per annum

    b $400 invested for five years at the rate of 8% per annum

    c $700 invested for two years at the rate of 15% per annum

    d $800 borrowed for eight years at the rate of 7% per annum

    e $5000 borrowed for 15 months at the rate of 5.5% per annum.

7 How much will you have in the bank if you invest $500 for four years at 3% interest, compounded annually?

8 Mrs Genaro owns a small business. She borrows $18 500 dollars from the bank to finance some new equipment. She repays the loan in full after two years. If the bank charged her compound interest at the rate of 21% per annum, how much did she owe them after two years?

17.3 Buying and selling

- The amount a business pays for an item is called the cost price. The price they sell it to the public for is called the selling price. The amount the seller adds onto the cost price to make a selling price is called a mark up. For example, a shopkeeper may buy an item for $2 and mark it up by 50 cents to sell it for $2.50.
- The difference between the cost price and the selling price is called the profit (if it is higher than the cost price) or the loss (if it is lower than the cost price).
  - Profit = selling price − cost price.
  - Loss = cost price − selling price.
- The rate of profit (or loss) is the percentage profit (or loss). Rate of profit (or loss) = $\dfrac{\text{profit (or loss)}}{\text{cost price}} \times 100\%$.
- A discount is an intentional reduction in the price of an item.
  Discount = original selling price − new marked price.
- The rate of discount is a percentage. Rate of discount = $\dfrac{\text{discount}}{\text{original selling price}} \times 100\%$.

Exercise 17.3

1 Find the cost price in each of the following:

    a selling price $120, profit 20%

    b selling price $230, profit 15%

    c selling price $289, loss 15%

    d selling price $600, loss $33\frac{1}{3}\%$.

2 Find the cost price of an article sold at $360 with a profit of 20%.

3 If a shopkeeper sells an article for $440 and loses 12% on the sale, find his cost price.

4 A dentist offers a 5% discount to patients who pay their accounts in cash within a week. How much will someone with an account of $67.80 pay if they pay promptly in cash?

5 Calculate the new selling price of each item with the following discounts.

  a $199 discount 10%

  b $45.50 discount 12%

  c $1020 discount $5\frac{1}{2}$%

Mixed exercise

1 Nerina earns $19.50 per hour. How many hours does she need to work to earn:

  a $234

  b $780

  c $497.25?

2 A mechanic works a 38-hour week for a basic wage of $28 per hour. Overtime is paid at time and a half on weekdays and double time on weekends. Calculate his gross earnings for a week if he works his normal hours plus:

  a three hours overtime on Thursday

  b one extra hour per day for the whole week

  c two hours overtime on Tuesday and $1\frac{1}{2}$ hours overtime on Saturday.

3 Jamira earns a monthly salary of $5234.

  a What is her annual gross salary?

  b She pays 12% tax and has a further $456.90 deducted from her monthly salary. Calculate her net monthly income.

4 A $10 000 investment earns interest at a rate of 3% p.a. This table compares the simple and compound interest.

Years	1	2	3	4	5	6	7	8
Simple interest	300	600						
Compound interest	300	609						

  a Copy and complete the table.

  b What is the difference between the simple interest and compound interest earned after five years?

  c Draw a bar chart to compare the value of the investment after one, five and 10 years for both types of interest. Comment on what your graph shows about the difference between simple and compound interest.

5 Find the selling price of an article that was bought for $750 and sold at a profit of 15%.

6 Calculate the selling price of an item of merchandise bought for $3000 and sold at a profit of 12%.

7 A gallery owner displays paintings for artists. She puts a 150% mark up on the price asked by the artist to cover her expenses and make a profit. An artist supplies three paintings at the prices listed below. For each one, calculate the mark up in dollars, and the selling price the gallery owner would charge.

    a Painting A, $890

    b Painting B, $1300

    c Painting C, $12 000

8 An art collector wants to buy paintings A and B (from question 7). He agrees to pay cash on condition that the gallery owner gives him a 12% discount on the selling price of the paintings.

    a What price will he pay?

    b What percentage profit does the gallery owner make on the sale?

9 A boy bought a bicycle for $500. After using it for two years, he sold it at a loss of 15%. Calculate the selling price.

10 It is found that an article is being sold at a loss of 12%. The cost of the article was $240. Calculate the selling price.

11 A woman makes dresses. Her total costs for ten dresses were $377. At what price should she sell the dresses to make 15% profit?

12 Sal wants to buy a used scooter. The cash price is $495. To buy on credit, she has to pay a 20% deposit and then 24 monthly instalments of $25 each. How much will she save by paying cash?

18 Curved graphs

18.1 Drawing quadratic graphs (the parabola)

- The highest power of a quadratic graph is two.
- The general formula for a quadratic graph is $y = ax^2 + bx + c$
- The axis of symmetry of the graph divides the parabola into two symmetrical halves.
- The turning point is the point at which the graph changes direction. This point is also called the vertex of the graph.
  - If the value of a in the general quadratic formula is positive, the parabola will be a 'valley shape' and the turning point a minimum value.
  - If the value of a in the general quadratic formula is negative, the parabola will be a 'hill shape' and the turning point a maximum value.

Exercise 18.1

Remember, the constant term (c in the general formula) is the y-intercept.

1 Copy and complete the following tables. Plot all the graphs onto the same set of axes. Use values of -12 to 12 on the y-axis.

a

x		−3	−2	−1	0	1	2	3
$y = -x^2 + 2$								

b

x		−3	−2	−1	0	1	2	3
$y = x^2 - 3$								

c

x		−3	−2	−1	0	1	2	3
$y = -x^2 - 2$								

d

x		−3	−2	−1	0	1	2	3
$y = -x^2 - 3$								

e

x		−3	−2	−1	0	1	2	3
$y = x^2 + \dfrac{1}{2}$								

2 Match each of the five parabolas shown here to one of the equations given.

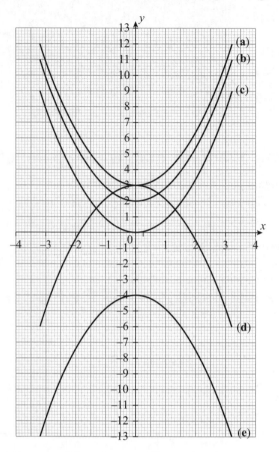

$$y = -4 - x^2 \qquad y = -x^2 + 3 \qquad y = 3 + x^2 \qquad y = x^2 + 2 \qquad y = x^2$$

3 Copy and complete the table of values for each of the equations given below. Plot the points on separate pairs of axes and join them, with a smooth curve, to draw the graph of the equation.

a

x	−2	−1	0	1	2	3	4	5
$y = x^2 - 3x + 2$								

b

x	−3	−2	−1	0	1	2	3
$y = x^2 - 2x - 1$							

c

x	−2	−1	0	1	2	3	4	5	6
$y = -x^2 + 4x + 1$									

4 Draw and label sketch graphs of the following functions.

    a $y = x^2 + 3x$ **b** $y = x^2 - x + 1$ **c** $y = -x^2 + 5x - 2$

5 A toy rocket is thrown up into the air. The graph below shows its path.

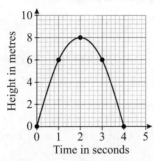

a What is the greatest height the rocket reaches?

b How long did it take for the rocket to reach this height?

c How high did the rocket reach in the first second?

d For how long was the rocket in the air?

e Estimate for how long the rocket was higher than 3 m above ground.

18.2 Drawing reciprocal graphs (the hyperbola)

- The general formula for a hyperbola graph is $y = \dfrac{a}{x}$ or $xy = a$.
- $x \neq 0$ and $y \neq 0$.
- The x-axis and the y-axis are asymptotes. This means the graph approaches the x-axis and the y-axis but never intersects with them.
- The graph is symmetrical about the $y = x$ or $y = -x$ line.

> **Tip**
>
> Reciprocal equations have a constant product. This means in $xy = a$, x and y are variables but a is a constant.

Exercise 18.2

1 Draw graphs for the following reciprocal graphs. Plot at least three points in each of the two quadrants and join them up with a smooth curve.

    a $xy = 5$ **b** $y = \dfrac{16}{x}$ **c** $xy = 9$

    d $y = -\dfrac{8}{x}$ **e** $y = -\dfrac{4}{x}$

2 The length and width of a certain rectangle can only be a whole number of metres. The area of the rectangle is 24 m².

    a Draw a table that shows all the possible combinations of measurements for the length and width of the rectangle.

    b Plot your values from (**a**) as points on a graph.

    c Join the points with a smooth curve. What does this graph represent?

    d Assuming, now, that the length and width of the rectangle can take any positive values that give an area of 24 m², use your graph to find the width if the length is 7 m.

18.3 Using graphs to solve quadratic equations

- If a quadratic equation has real roots the graph of the equation will intersect with the x-axis. This is where $y = 0$.
- To solve quadratic equations graphically, read off the x-coordinates of the points for a given y-value.

Exercise 18.3

1 Use this graph of the relationship $y = x^2 - x - 6$ to solve the following equations.

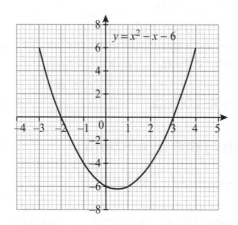

Tip

For part (c) you might find it helpful to rearrange the equation so the left-hand side matches the equation of the graph, i.e. subtract 6 from both sides.

    a $x^2 - x - 6 = 0$ **b** $x^2 - x - 6 = -4$ **c** $x^2 - x = 12$

2 a Draw the graph of $y = -x^2 - x + 2$ for values of x from -3 to 2.

    b Use your graph to find the approximate solutions to the equations:

       i $-x^2 - x + 2 = 0$

       ii $-x^2 - x + 2 = 1$

      iii $-x^2 - x + 2 = -2$

3 a Use an interval of $-4 \leqslant x \leqslant 5$ on the x-axis to draw the graph $y = x^2 - x - 6$.

    b Use the graph to solve the following equations:

       i $-6 = x^2 - x - 6$

      ii $x^2 - x - 6 = 0$

      iii $x^2 - x = 12$

18.4 Using graphs to solve simultaneous linear and non-linear equations

- The solution is the point where the graphs intersect.

Exercise 18.4

1 Draw these pairs of graphs and find the points where they intersect.

    a $y = \dfrac{4}{x}$ and $y = 2x + 2$

    b $y = x^2 + 2x - 3$ and $y = -x + 1$

    c $y = -x^2 + 4$ and $y = \dfrac{3}{x}$

2 Use a graphical method to solve the following equations simultaneously.

a $y = 2x^2 + 3x - 2$ and $y = x + 2$

b $y = x^2 + 2x$ and $y = -x + 4$

c $y = -2x^2 + 2x + 4$ and $y = -2x - 4$

d $y = -0.5x^2 + x + 1.5$ and $y = \dfrac{1}{2}x$

Mixed exercise

1 a Copy and complete the tables below for the following equations, $y = x^2 - 8$ and $y = 2x - 3$. Then plot and draw the graphs of the equations onto the same pair of axes.

x		-3	-2	-1	0	1	2	3	4
$y = x^2 - 8$									

x		-1	-2	-1	0	1	2	3	4
$y = 2x - 3$									

b Using your graph, determine the value of x when $x^2 - 8 = 2x - 3$.

c What is the minimum value of $y = x^2 - 8$?

2 The dotted line on the grid below is the axis of symmetry for the given hyperbola.

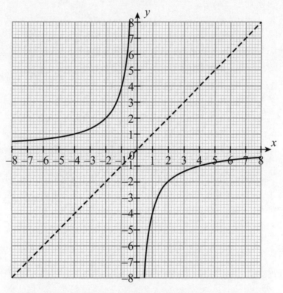

a Give the equation for the hyperbola.

b Give the equation for the given line of symmetry.

c Copy the diagram into your workbook and draw in the other line of symmetry, giving the equation for this line.

3 Look at these sketch graphs. For each one, write the general form of its equation. Use letters to represent any constant values if you need to.

a

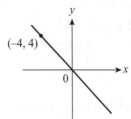

(–4, 4)

b

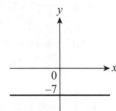

–7

c

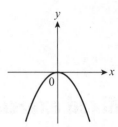

d

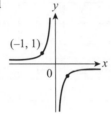

(–1, 1)

e

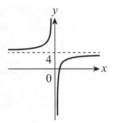

4

19 Symmetry

19.1 Symmetry in two dimensions

- Two-dimensional (flat) shapes have line symmetry if you are able to draw a line through the shape so that one side of the line is the mirror image (reflection) of the other side. There may be more than one possible line of symmetry in a shape.

- If you rotate (turn) a shape around a fixed point and it fits on to itself during the rotation, then it has rotational symmetry. The number of times the shape fits on to its original position during a rotation is called the order of rotational symmetry.

If a shape can only fit back into itself after a full 360° rotation, it has no rotational symmetry.

Exercise 19.1

1 For each of the following shapes:

    a copy the shape and draw in any lines of symmetry

    b determine the order of rotational symmetry.

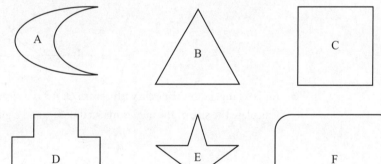

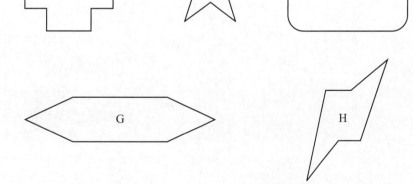

2 **a** How many lines of symmetry does a rhombus have? Draw a diagram to show your solution.

    b What is the order of rotational symmetry of a rhombus?

3 Draw a quadrilateral that has no lines of symmetry and no rotational symmetry.

19.2 Angle relationships in circles

- When a triangle is drawn in a semi-circle, so that one side is the diameter and the vertex opposite the diameter touches the circumference, the angle of the vertex opposite the diameter is a right angle (90°).
- Where a tangent touches a circle, the radius drawn to the same point meets the tangent at 90°.

Exercise 19.2

The angle relationships for triangles, quadrilaterals and parallel lines (chapter 3), as well as Pythagoras' theorem (chapter 11), may be needed to solve circle problems.

1 Given that O is the centre of the circle, calculate the value of angle BAD with reasons.

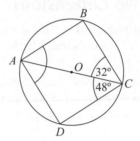

2 DC is a tangent to the circle with centre O. Find the size of angle DCA.

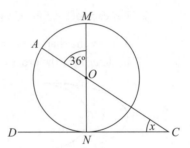

3 EC is a tangent to the circle with centre O. AB is a straight line and angle $CBD = 37°$. Calculate the size of the angles marked w, x, y and z giving reasons for each.

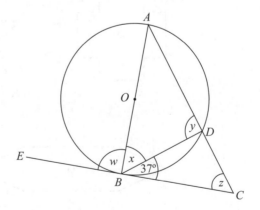

Mixed exercise

1 Here are five shapes.

a   b   c   d   e

For each one:

   i indicate the axes of symmetry (if any)
   ii state the order of rotational symmetry.

2 Find the sizes of angles *a* to *e* in the following figure.

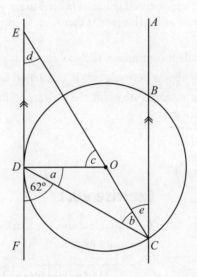

20 Histograms and frequency distribution diagrams

20.1 Histograms

- A histogram is a specialised graph. It is used to show grouped numerical data using a continuous scale on the horizontal axis. (This means there are no gaps in between the data categories – where one ends, the other begins).
- Because the scale is continuous, each column is drawn above a particular class interval.
- A gap will only appear between bars if an interval has a frequency of zero.
- When the class intervals are equal, the bars are all the same width and it is common practice to (label) the vertical scale as frequency.

Exercise 20.1

1 The table shows the marks obtained by a number of students for English and Mathematics in a mock exam.

Remember there can be no gaps between the bars: use the upper and lower bounds of each class interval to prevent gaps.

Marks class interval	English frequency	Mathematics frequency
1–10	0	0
11–20	3	2
21–30	7	5
31–40	4	6
41–50	29	34
51–60	51	48
61–70	40	45
71–80	12	6
81–90	3	2
91–100	1	2

REWIND

You met the mode in chapter 12. ◄

a Draw two separate histograms to show the distribution of marks for English and Mathematics.

b What is the modal class for English?

c What is the modal class for Mathematics?

d Write a few sentences comparing the students' performance in English and Mathematics.

2 Study this graph and answer the questions about it.

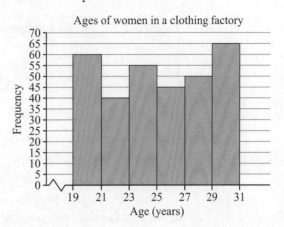

a How do you know this is a histogram and not a bar graph?

b How many women aged 23–25 work in the clothing factory?

c How many women work in the factory altogether?

d What is the modal class of this data?

e Explain why there is a broken line on the horizontal axis.

Mixed exercise

1 This partially completed histogram shows the heights of trees in a section of tropical forest.

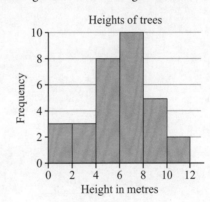

a A scientist measured five more trees and their heights were: 2.09 m, 3.34 m, 6.45 m, 9.26 m and 3.88 m. Redraw the graph to include this data.

b How many trees in this sector of forest are ⩾ 6 m tall?

c What is the modal class of tree heights?

2 A nurse measured the masses of a sample of students in a high school and drew the following table.

Mass (kg)	Frequency
$54 \leqslant m < 56$	4
$56 \leqslant m < 58$	7
$58 \leqslant m < 60$	13
$60 \leqslant m < 62$	19
$62 \leqslant m < 64$	11

a Draw a histogram to show the distribution of masses.
b What is the modal mass?
c What percentage of students weighed less than 56 kg?
d What is the maximum possible range of the masses?

21 Ratio, rate and proportion

21.1 Working with ratio

- A ratio is a comparison of two or more quantities measured in the same units. In general, a ratio is written in the form $a:b$.
- Ratios should always be given in their simplest form. To express a ratio in simplest form, divide or multiply by the same factor.
- Quantities can be shared in a given ratio. To do this you need to work out the number of equal parts in the ratio and then work out the value of each share. For example, a ratio of $3:2$ means that there are 5 equal parts. One share is $\frac{3}{5}$ of the total and the other is $\frac{2}{5}$ of the total.

Remember, simplest form is also called 'lowest terms'.

Exercise 21.1

1 Express the following as ratios in their simplest form.

    a $120:150$ **b** $2\frac{3}{4}:3\frac{2}{3}$ **c** $1\frac{1}{2}$ hours : 15 minutes

    d 125 litres to 350 litres   **e** 45 cents to \$2   **f** 175 cm to 2 m

    g 600 g to three kilograms   **h** 50 mm to a metre   **i** 12.5 g to 50 g

    j 3 cm to 25 mm   **k** 200 ml of 3 l

2 Find the value of x in each of the following.

    a $2:3 = 6:x$ **b** $2:5 = x:10$ **c** $2:x = 3:24$ **d** $x:12 = 2:8$

    e $10:15 = x:6$ **f** $\frac{2}{7} = \frac{x}{4}$ **g** $\frac{5}{x} = \frac{16}{6}$ **h** $\frac{x}{4} = \frac{10}{15}$

    i $\frac{x}{21} = \frac{1}{3}$ **j** $\frac{5}{x} = \frac{3}{8}$

Tip

You can cross multiply to make an equation and solve for x.

3 Nesta and Tyson shared \$12 000 in the ratio $3:2$. Calculate each person's share.

4 Divide 350 sheets of paper in the ratio $2:5$.

5 A length of rope 160 cm long must be cut into two parts so that the lengths are in the ratio $3:5$. What are the lengths of the parts?

6 To make salad dressing, you mix oil and vinegar in the ratio $2:3$. Calculate how much oil and how much vinegar you will need to make the following amounts of salad dressing:

    a 50 ml   **b** 600 ml   **c** 750 ml.

7 The sizes of three angles of a triangle are in the ratio $A:B:C = 2:1:3$. What is the size of each angle?

8 A metal disc consists of three parts silver and two parts copper (by mass). If the disc has a mass of 1350 mg, how much silver does it contain?

21.2 Ratio and scale

- Scale is a ratio. It can be expressed as
  length on the drawing : real length.
- All ratio scales must be expressed in the form of $1:n$ or $n:1$.
- To change a ratio so that one part = 1, you need to divide both parts by the number that you want to be expressed as 1. For example with $2:7$, if you want the 2 to be expressed as 1, you divide both parts by 2. The result is $1:3.5$.

Tip

With reductions (such as maps) the scale will be in the form $1:n$, where $n > 1$. With enlargements the scale will be in the form $n:1$, where $n > 1$. n may not be a whole number.

Exercise 21.2 A

1 Write these ratios in the form of $1:n$.

   a 4:9   **b** 400 m : 1.3 km   **c** 50 minutes : $1\frac{1}{2}$ hours

2 Write these ratios in the form of $n:1$.

   a 12:8   **b** 2 m : 40 cm   **c** 2.5 g to 500 mg

Exercise 21.2 B

1 The distance between two points on a map with a scale of $1:2\,000\,000$ is 120 mm. What is the distance between the two points in reality? Give your answer in kilometres.

2 A plan is drawn using a scale of $1:500$. If the length of a wall on the plan is 6 cm, how long is the wall in reality?

3 Miguel makes a scale drawing to solve a trigonometry problem. 1 cm on his drawing represents 2 m in real life. He wants to show a 10 m long ladder placed 7 m from the foot of a wall.

   a What length will the ladder be in the diagram?
   b How far will it be from the foot of the wall in the diagram?

4 A map has a scale of $1:700\,000$.

   a What does a scale of $1:700\,000$ mean?
   b Copy and complete this table using the map scale.

Map distance (mm)	10		50	80		
Actual distance (km)		50			1200	1500

5 Mary has a rectangular picture 35 mm wide and 37 mm high. She enlarges it on the photocopier so that the enlargement is 14 cm wide.

   a What is the scale factor of the enlargement?
   b What is the height of her enlarged picture?
   c In the original picture, a fence was 30 mm long. How long will this fence be on the enlarged picture?

21.3 Rates

- A rate compares two quantities measured in different units. For example speed is a rate that compares kilometres travelled per hour.
- Rates can be simplified just like ratios. They can also be expressed in the form of $1:n$.
- You solve rate problems in the same way that you solved ratio and proportion problems. Use the unitary or ratio methods.

Tip

The word 'per' is often used in a rates. Per can mean 'for every', 'in each', 'out of every', or 'out of' depending on the context.

Remember, speed is a very important rate.

$$\text{speed} = \frac{\text{distance}}{\text{time}}$$
$$\text{distance} = \text{speed} \times \text{time}$$
$$\text{time} = \frac{\text{distance}}{\text{speed}}$$

Exercise 21.3

1. At a market, milk costs $1.95 per litre. How much milk can you buy for $50?

2. Sam travels a distance of 437 km and uses 38 litres of petrol. Express his petrol consumption as a rate in km/l.

3. Calculate the average speed of the following vehicles.

   a. A car that travels 196 km in 2.5 hours.
   b. A plane that travels 650 km in one hour 15 minutes.
   c. A train that travels 180 km in 45 minutes.

4. How long would it take to travel:

   a. 400 km at 80 km/h   b. 900 km at 95 km/h
   c. 1800 km at 45 km/h   d. 500 m at 7 km/h

5. How far would you travel in $2\frac{1}{2}$ hours at these speeds?

   a. 60 km/h   b. 120 km/h
   c. 25 metres per minute   d. two metres per second

6. A gold bar has a volume of 725 cm³ and a mass of 14.5 kg. Given that density $= \dfrac{\text{mass}}{\text{volume}}$, calculate the density of the gold bar in g/cm³.

21.4 Kinematic graphs

- Distance–time graphs show the connection between the distance an object has travelled and the time taken to travel that distance. They are also called travel graphs.
- Time is normally shown along the horizontal axis because it is the independent variable. Distance is shown on the vertical axis because it is the dependent variable.
- You can determine speed on a distance–time graph by looking at the slope (steepness) of the line. The steeper the line, the greater the speed; a straight line indicates constant speed; upward and downward slopes represent movement in opposite directions; and a horizontal line represents no movement:
  - Average speed $= \dfrac{\text{distance travelled}}{\text{time taken}} = \dfrac{\text{change in } y\text{-coordinate}}{\text{change in } x\text{-coordinate}}$

Exercise 21.4

1 The graph below shows the distance covered by a vehicle in a six-hour period.

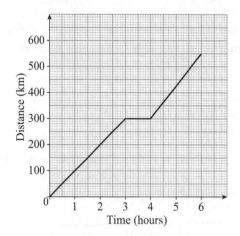

   a Use the graph to find the distance covered after:
      i one hour   **ii** two hours   **iii** three hours.
   b Calculate the average speed of the vehicle during the first three hours.
   c Describe what the graph shows between hour three and four.
   d What distance did the vehicle cover during the last two hours of the journey?
   e What was its average speed during the last two hours of the journey?

2 Dabilo and Pam live 200 km apart from each other. They decide to meet up at a shopping centre in-between their homes on a Saturday. Pam travels by bus and Dabilo catches a train. The graph shows both journeys.

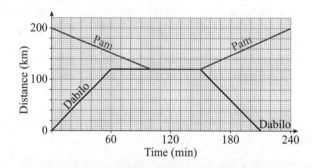

   a How much time did Dabilo spend on the train?
   b How much time did Pam spend on the bus?
   c At what speed did the train travel for the first hour?
   d How far was the shopping centre from:
      i Dabilo's home?   **ii** Pam's home?
   e What was the average speed of the bus from Pam's home to the shopping centre?
   f How long did Dabilo have to wait before Pam arrived?
   g How long did the two girls spend together?
   h How much faster was Pam's journey on the way home?
   i If they left home at 8:00 a.m., what time did each girl return home after the day's outing?

21.5 Proportion

- Proportion is a constant ratio between the corresponding elements of two sets.
- When quantities are in direct proportion they increase or decrease at the same rate. The graph of a directly proportionate relationship is a straight line passing through the origin.
- When quantities are inversely proportional, one increases as the other decreases. The graph of an inversely proportional relationship is a curve.
- The unitary method is useful for solving ratio and proportion problems. This method involves finding the value of one unit (of work, time, etc.) and using that value to find the value of a number of units.

Tip

If x and y are directly proportional, then $\frac{x}{y}$ is the same for various values of x and y.

Exercise 21.5

1 Determine whether A and B are directly proportional in each case.

a
A	2	4	6
B	300	600	900

b
A	2	5	8
B	2	10	15

c
A	1	2	3	4
B	0.1	0.2	0.3	0.4

2 A textbook costs $25.

   a What is the price of seven books?
   b What is the price of ten books?

3 Find the cost of five identically priced items if seven items cost $17.50.

4 If a 3.5 m tall pole casts a 10.5 m shadow, find the length of the shadow cast by a 20 m tall pole at the same time.

5 A car travels a distance of 225 km in three hours at a constant speed.

   a What distance will it cover in one hour at the same speed?
   b How far will it travel in five hours at the same speed?
   c How long will it take to travel 250 km at the same speed?

6 A truck uses 20 litres of diesel to travel 240 kilometres.

   a How much diesel will it use to travel 180 km at the same rate?
   b How far could the truck travel on 45 litres of diesel at the same rate?

7 It takes one employee ten days to complete a project. If another employee joins him, it only takes five days. Five employees can complete the job in two days.

   a Describe this relationship.
   b How long would it take to complete the project with:
      i four employees
      ii 20 employees?

8 At a campsite, ten people have enough fresh water to last them for six days at a set rate per person.

    a How long would the water last, if there were only five people drinking it at the same rate?

    b Another two people join the group. How long will the water last if it is used at the same rate?

9 Nick took four hours to complete a journey at 110 km/h. Marie did the same journey at 80 km/h. How long did it take her?

10 A plane travelling at an average speed of 1000 km/h takes 12 hours to complete a journey. How fast would it need to travel to cover the same distance in ten hours?

Mixed exercise

1 Express the following as ratios in their simplest form.

    a $3\frac{1}{2} : 4\frac{3}{4}$ **b** 5 ml to 2.5 litres   **c** 125 g to 1 kilogram

2 Divide 600 in these ratios.

    a $7:3$ **b** $7:5$ **c** $7:13$ **d** $7:7$

3 A builder mixes sand and cement in the ratio $4:1$ to make mortar for a wall. How much cement will be needed for the following amounts of sand?

    a four spadefuls   **b** two bags   **c** $1\frac{1}{2}$ wheelbarrows full

4 A triangle of perimeter 360 mm has side lengths in the ratio $3:5:4$.

    a Find the lengths of the sides.
    b Is the triangle right-angled? Give a reason for your answer.

5 A model of a car is built to a scale of $1:50$. If the real car is 2.5 m long, what is the length of the model in centimetres?

6 On a floor plan of a school, 2 cm represents 1 m in the real school. What is the scale of the plan?

7 An athlete runs 100 m in 9.9 seconds. Express this speed in:

    a metres per second   **b** kilometres per hour.

8 A car travels at an average speed of 85 km/h.

    a What distance will the car travel in:

        i 1 hour   **ii** $4\frac{1}{2}$ hours   **iii** 15 minutes?

    b How long will it take the car to travel:
        i 30 km   **ii** 400 km   **iii** 100 km?

9 This travel graph shows the journey of a petrol tanker doing deliveries.

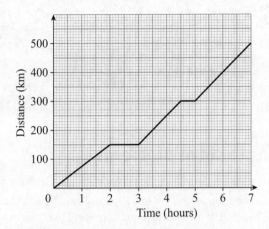

a What distance did the tanker travel in the first two hours?

b When did the tanker stop to make its first delivery? For how long was it stopped?

c Calculate the average speed of the tanker between the first and second stop on the route.

d What was the average speed of the tanker during the last two hours of the journey?

e How far did the tanker travel on this journey?

10 Nine students complete a task in three minutes. How long would it take six students to complete the same task if they worked at the same rate?

11 A cube with sides of 2 cm has a mass of 12 grams. Find the mass of another cube made of the same material if it has sides of 5 cm.

22 More equations, formulae and functions

22.1 Setting up equations to solve problems

- You can set up your own equations and use them to solve problems that have a number as an answer.
- The first step in setting up an equation is to work out what needs to be calculated. Represent this amount using a variable (usually x). You then construct an equation using the information you are given and solve it to find the answer.

> **Tip**
> There is usually one word or short statement in the problem that means 'equal to'. Examples are: total, gives, the answer is, the result is, product of is, and sum of is.

Exercise 22.1 A

In each of the following, set up an equation and solve it to find the unknown value.

1 When five is added to a number, the result is 14. Find the number.

2 If a number is decreased by seven the answer is 19. What is the number?

3 Twice a certain number increased by 12 is 280. What is the number?

4 The product of six and a certain number is equal to four times the number plus 16. What is the number?

5 A third of a number is equal to half of the same number *after* it has been decreased by two. Determine the number.

6 The difference between two numbers is five. Three times the greater number is equal to 10 times the smaller plus one. Find the numbers.

7 Half of a number is subtracted from four times itself to get seven. What is the number?

8 The sum of two numbers is 100. Twice one number is equal to the other number plus 20. Find the numbers.

> **Tip**
> When you have to give a formula, you should express it in simplest terms by collecting like terms.

Exercise 22.1 B

1 A rectangle is 4 cm longer than it is wide. If the rectangle is x cm long, write down:

    a the width (in terms of x)
    b a formula for calculating the perimeter (P) of the rectangle.
    c a formula for finding the area (A) of the rectangle in simplest terms.

2 Three numbers are represented by x, $3x$ and $x + 2$.

    a Write a formula for finding the sum (S) of the three numbers.
    b Write a formula for finding the mean (M) of the three numbers.

3 The smallest of three consecutive numbers is x.

    a Express the other two numbers in terms of x.

    b Write a formula for finding the sum (S) of the numbers.

4 Sammy is two years older than Max. Tayo is three years younger than Max. If Max is x years old, write down:

    a Sammy's age in terms of x

    b Tayo's age in term of x

    c a formula for finding the combined ages of the three boys.

Exercise 22.1 C

1 There are 12 more girls than boys in a class of 40 students. How many boys are there?

2 A rectangle has an area of $36\,cm^2$ and the breadth is $4\,cm$. Find the length of the rectangle.

3 There are ten times as many silver cars than red cars in a parking area. If there 88 silver and red cars altogether, find the number of cars of each colour.

4 Nadira is 25 years younger than her father. Nadira's mother is two years younger than her father. Together Nadira, her mother and father have a combined age of 78. Work out their ages.

5 The perimeter of a parallelogram is $104\,cm$. If the length is three times the breadth, calculate the dimensions of the parallelogram.

6 Jess thinks of a number. When she doubles it and then adds five, she gets the same answer as when she subtracts it from two.

    a Make an equation to represent this problem. Let the unknown number be x.

    b Solve your equation to find the number that Jess was thinking of.

7 A triangle has sides of $x\,cm$, $x + 4\,cm$ and $x + 8\,cm$.

    a Write a formula in terms of x for calculating P, the perimeter of the triangle.

    b Use your formula to find the lengths of each side of a triangle when:

        i $P = 45\,cm$ **ii** $P = 23.25\,cm$.

Mixed exercise

1 A certain number increased by six is equal to twice the same number decreased by four. What is the number?

2 If three times a number is increased by five, the result is 17. What is the number?

3 Three times a number decreased by two is equal to the sum of the number and six. Determine the number.

4 Cedric has \$16 more than Nathi. Together they have \$150. How much does each person have?

5 A woman has a certain number of cakes to sell. She sells all except 15 for $6 each and receives $240. How many cakes did she have to sell?

6 Two items together costs $60. If a discount of 25% is given on one item, then the two items together cost $50. What was the original price of each item?

7 A rectangle of area A has sides of $x + 3$ and $x - 2$.

   a Write a formula in terms of x for finding P, the perimeter of the rectangle.
   b Find the length of each side if the rectangle has a perimeter of 98.

23

Vectors and transformations

23.1 Simple plane transformations

- A transformation is a change in the position or size of a point or a shape.
- There are four basic transformations: reflection, rotation, translation and enlargement.
  - The original shape is called the object (O) and the transformed shape is called the image (O').
- A reflection flips the shape over.
  - Under reflection, every point on a shape is reflected in a mirror line to produce a mirror-image of the object. Points on the object and corresponding points on the image are the same distance from the mirror line, when you measure the distance perpendicular to the mirror line.
  - To describe a reflection you need to give the equation of the mirror line.
- A rotation turns the shape around a point.
  - The point about which a shape is rotated is called the centre of rotation. The shape may be rotated clockwise or anticlockwise.
  - To describe a rotation you need to give the centre of rotation and the angle and direction of turn.
- A translation is a slide movement.
  - Under translation, every point on the object moves the same distance in the same direction to form the image. Translation involves moving the shape sideways and/or up and down. The translation can therefore be described using a column vector $\begin{pmatrix} x \\ y \end{pmatrix}$ where x is the movement to the side (along the x-axis) and y is the movement up or down. The sign of the x or y value gives you the direction of the translation. Positive means to the right or up and negative means to the left or down.
- An enlargement involves changing the size of an object to produce an image that is similar in shape to the object.
  - The enlargement factor = $\dfrac{\text{length of a side on the image}}{\text{length of the corresponding side on the object}}$. When an object is enlarged from a fixed point, it has a centre of enlargement. The centre of enlargement determines the position of the image. Lines drawn through corresponding points on the object and the image will meet at the centre of enlargement.
- The transformations above can be combined.

Tip

Reflection and rotation change the position and orientation of the object while translation only changes the position. Enlargement changes the size of the object to produce the image but its orientation is not changed.

Exercise 23.1 A

You will need square paper for this exercise.

1 Draw and label any rectangle $ABCD$.

  a Rotate the rectangle clockwise 90° about point D. Label the image $A'B'C'D'$.
  b Reflect $A'B'C'D'$ about $B'D'$.

2 Make a copy of the diagram below and carry out the following transformations.

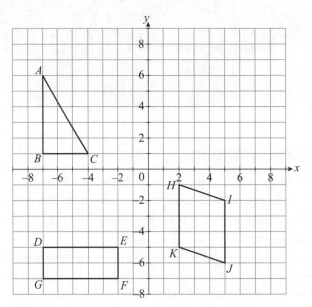

a Translate triangle *ABC* three units to the right and four units up. Label the image correctly.

b Reflect rectangle *DEFG* about the line $y = -3$. Label the image correctly.

c **i** Rotate parallelogram *HIJK* 90° anticlockwise about point $(2, -1)$.

  ii Translate the image *H'I'J'K'* one unit left and five units up.

3 Make a copy of the diagram below and carry out the following transformations.

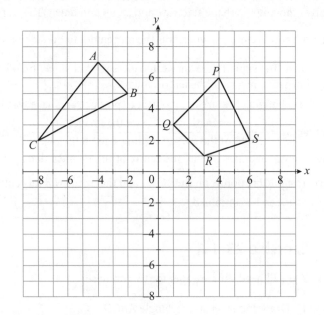

a Triangle *ABC* is translated using the column vector $\begin{pmatrix} 10 \\ -9 \end{pmatrix}$ to form the image *A'B'C'*. Draw and label the image.

b Quadrilateral *PQRS* is reflected in the *y*-axis and then translated using the column vector $\begin{pmatrix} 0 \\ 6 \end{pmatrix}$. Draw the resultant image *P'Q'R'S'*.

4 For each of the reflections shown in the diagram, give the equation of the mirror line.

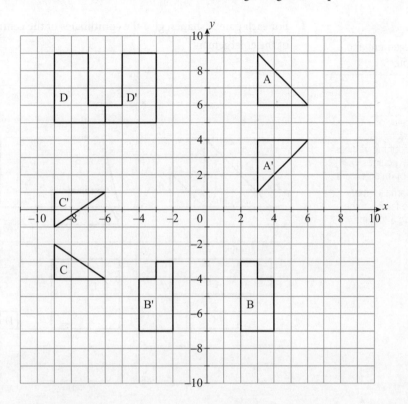

5 Copy the diagram for question 4 and draw the reflection of each shape (A–D) in the *x*-axis.

6 In each of the following, fully describe at least two different transformations that map the object onto its image.

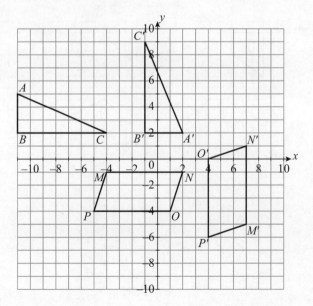

REWIND

You dealt with enlargement and scale factors in chapter 21. ◀

You can find the centre of enlargement by drawing lines through the corresponding vertices on the two shapes. The lines will meet at the centre of enlargement.

When the image is smaller than the object, the scale factor of the 'enlargement' will be a fraction.

Exercise 23.1 B

1 For each pair of shapes, give the coordinates of the centre of enlargement and the scale factor of the enlargement.

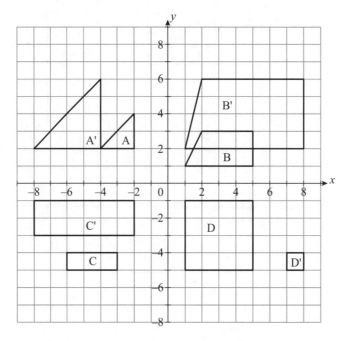

2 Copy each shape onto squared grid paper. Using point X as a centre of enlargement, draw the image of each shape under an enlargement with scale factor:

i 2   ii $\frac{1}{2}$

a 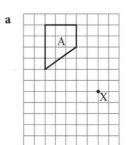   b 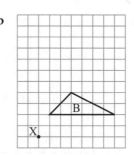   c 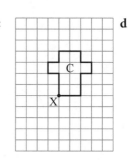   d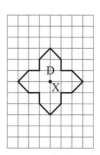

Exercise 23.1 C

1 Triangle ABC is to be reflected in the y-axis and its image triangle $A'B'C'$ is then to be reflected in the x-axis to form triangle $A''B''C''$.

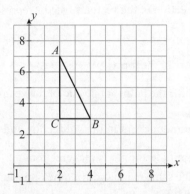

    a Draw a set of axes, extending them into the negative direction. Copy triangle ABC onto your grid and draw the transformations described.

    b Describe the single transformation that maps triangle ABC directly onto triangle $A''B''C''$.

2 Shape A is to be enlarged by a scale factor of two, using the origin as the centre of enlargement, to get shape B. Shape B is then translated, using the column vector $\begin{pmatrix} -8 \\ 1 \end{pmatrix}$, to get shape C.

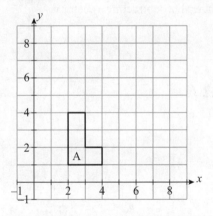

    a Draw a set of axes, extending the x-axis into the negative direction. Copy shape A onto your grid and draw the two transformations described.

    b What single transformation would have the same results as these two transformations?

3 A trapezium $ABCD$ with its vertices at coordinates $A\,(2, 4)$, $B\,(3, 4)$, $C\,(3, 1)$ and $D\,(1, 1)$ is to be reflected in the line $x = 4$. The image is to be reflected in the line $y = 5$.

    a Draw the shape and show its position after each reflection. Label the final image F'.

    b Describe the single transformation you could use to transform $ABCD$ to F'.

23.2 Vectors

- A vector is a quantity that has both magnitude (size) and direction.
- Vectors can be represented by line segments. The length of the line represents the magnitude of the vector and the arrow on the line represents the direction of the vector. A vector represented by line segment AB starts at A and extends in the direction of B.
- The notation $\mathbf{a}$, $\mathbf{b}$, $\mathbf{c}$ or $\mathbf{AB}$, $\overrightarrow{AB}$ is used for vectors.
- Vectors can also be written as column vectors in the form $\begin{pmatrix} x \\ y \end{pmatrix}$.

  A column vector represents a translation (how the point at one end of the vector moves to get to the other end of the line).

  The column vector $\begin{pmatrix} 1 \\ 2 \end{pmatrix}$ represents a translation one unit in the x-direction and two units in the y-direction.

- Vectors are equal if they have the same magnitude and the same direction.
- The negative of a vector is the vector with the same magnitude but the opposite direction. So, the negative of $\mathbf{a}$ is $-\mathbf{a}$ and the negative of $\mathbf{AB}$ is $\mathbf{BA}$.
- Vectors cannot be multiplied by each other, but they can be multiplied by a scalar (a number).

  Multiplying any vector $\begin{pmatrix} x \\ y \end{pmatrix}$ by a scalar k, gives $\begin{pmatrix} kx \\ ky \end{pmatrix}$.

- Vectors can be added and subtracted using the 'nose-to-tail' method or triangle rule.

  $$\begin{pmatrix} x_1 \\ y_1 \end{pmatrix} + \begin{pmatrix} x_2 \\ y_2 \end{pmatrix} = \begin{pmatrix} x_1 + x_2 \\ y_1 + y_2 \end{pmatrix}.$$

  To subtract vectors, you need to remember that subtracting a vector is the same as adding its negative.

  So $(\mathbf{AB} - \mathbf{CA}) = \mathbf{AB} + \mathbf{AC}$.

Exercise 23.2 A

Remember, a scalar is a quantity without direction, basically just a number or measurement.

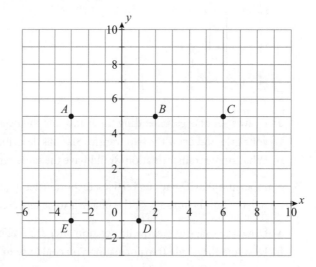

1 Using the points on the grid above, express each of the following as a column vector:

Remember, equal vectors have the same magnitude and direction; negative vectors have the same magnitude and opposite directions.

a $\overrightarrow{AB}$	**b** $\overrightarrow{BC}$	**c** $\overrightarrow{AE}$	**d** $\overrightarrow{BD}$
e $\overrightarrow{DB}$	**f** $\overrightarrow{EC}$	**g** $\overrightarrow{CD}$	**h** $\overrightarrow{BE}$

i What is the relationship between $\overrightarrow{BE}$ and $\overrightarrow{CD}$? **j** What is $\overrightarrow{AB} + \overrightarrow{BC}$?

k What is $\overrightarrow{AE} - \overrightarrow{AB}$? **l** Is $\overrightarrow{BC} = \overrightarrow{ED}$?

2 Represent the following vectors on squared paper.

a $\overrightarrow{AB} = \begin{pmatrix} 2 \\ 3 \end{pmatrix}$ **b** $\overrightarrow{CD} = \begin{pmatrix} -1 \\ 4 \end{pmatrix}$ **c** $\overrightarrow{EF} = \begin{pmatrix} 4 \\ 5 \end{pmatrix}$ **d** $\overrightarrow{GH} = \begin{pmatrix} 3 \\ -4 \end{pmatrix}$

3 Find the column vector that describes the translation from the object to its image in each of the following examples.

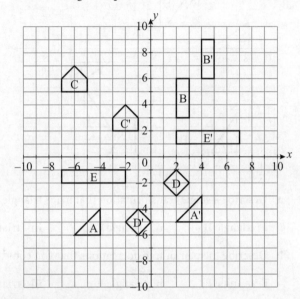

Exercise 23.2 B

1 Given that $\mathbf{a} = \begin{pmatrix} 1 \\ 3 \end{pmatrix}$, $\mathbf{b} = \begin{pmatrix} -2 \\ 4 \end{pmatrix}$ and $\mathbf{c} = \begin{pmatrix} 0 \\ -3 \end{pmatrix}$, find:

a $4\mathbf{b}$ **b** $2\mathbf{a}$ **c** $-4\mathbf{c}$ **d** $\mathbf{a} + \mathbf{b}$ **e** $\mathbf{b} + \mathbf{c}$
f $\mathbf{a} + \mathbf{b} + \mathbf{c}$ **g** $2\mathbf{a} + 3\mathbf{b}$ **h** $4\mathbf{b} - 2\mathbf{c}$ **i** $-4\mathbf{a} - 2\mathbf{b}$ **j** $2\mathbf{a} - 4\mathbf{b} + 2\mathbf{b}$

2 The diagram shows the pattern on a floor tile. The tiles are squares divided into four congruent triangles by the intersecting diagonals of each square.

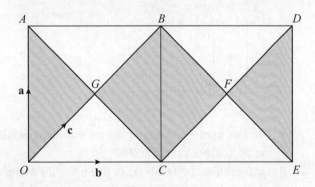

The vectors $\overrightarrow{OA} = \mathbf{a}$, $\overrightarrow{OC} = \mathbf{b}$ and $\overrightarrow{OG} = \mathbf{c}$ are shown. Use this information to write each of the following in terms of $\mathbf{a}$, $\mathbf{b}$ and $\mathbf{c}$.

a $\overrightarrow{DE}$ **b** $\overrightarrow{AD}$ **c** $\overrightarrow{AG}$ **d** $\overrightarrow{OB}$
e $\overrightarrow{OE}$ **f** $\overrightarrow{CD}$ **g** $\overrightarrow{BF} + \overrightarrow{FD}$ **h** $\overrightarrow{DE} + \overrightarrow{EF}$
i $4\overrightarrow{BF} - 3\overrightarrow{EF}$ **j** $\frac{1}{2}\overrightarrow{OC} + 3\overrightarrow{GB}$

Mixed exercise

1

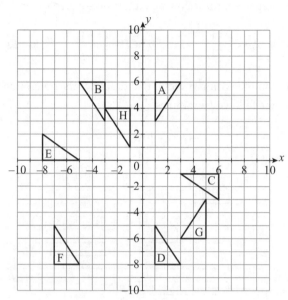

  a Describe a single transformation that maps triangle A onto:

   i triangle B   **ii** triangle C   **iii** triangle D.

  b Describe the pair of transformations that you could use to map triangle A onto:

   i triangle E   **ii** triangle F   **iii** triangle G   **iv** triangle H.

2 Sally translated parallelogram *DEFG* along the column vector $\begin{pmatrix} -4 \\ 5 \end{pmatrix}$ and then rotated it 90°

clockwise about the origin to get the image *D′E′F′G′* shown on the grid.

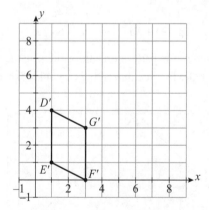

  a Draw a diagram and reverse the transformations Sally performed on the shape to show the original position of *DEFG*.

  b Enlarge *DEFG* by a scale factor of 2 using the origin as the centre of enlargement. Label your enlargement *D″E″F″G″*.

3 Square *ABCD* is shown on the grid.

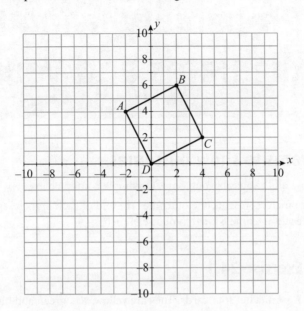

Onto a copy of the diagram, draw the following transformations and, in each case, give the coordinates of the new position of vertex *B*.

a Reflect *ABCD* about the line $x = -2$.

b Rotate *ABCD* 90° clockwise about the origin.

c Translate *ABCD* along the column vector $\begin{pmatrix} -3 \\ 2 \end{pmatrix}$.

d Enlarge *ABCD* by a scale factor of 1.5 using the origin as the centre of enlargement.

4 Given that $\mathbf{a} = \begin{pmatrix} 3 \\ 6 \end{pmatrix}$, $\mathbf{b} = \begin{pmatrix} 2 \\ -4 \end{pmatrix}$ and $\mathbf{c} = \begin{pmatrix} -2 \\ -4 \end{pmatrix}$,

a find:

   i $2\mathbf{a}$ **ii** $\mathbf{b} + \mathbf{c}$ **iii** $\mathbf{a} - \mathbf{b}$ **iv** $2\mathbf{a} + 3\mathbf{b}$

b Draw four separate vector diagrams on squared paper to represent:

   i $\mathbf{a}, 2\mathbf{a}$ **ii** $\mathbf{b}, \mathbf{c}, \mathbf{b} + \mathbf{c}$ **iii** $\mathbf{a}, \mathbf{b}, \mathbf{a} - \mathbf{b}$ **iv** $\mathbf{a}, \mathbf{b}, 2\mathbf{a} + 3\mathbf{b}$

24 Probability using tree diagrams and Venn diagrams

24.1 Using tree diagrams to show outcomes

- A probability tree shows all the possible outcomes for simple combined events.
- Each line segment or branch represents one outcome. The end of each branch segment is labelled with the outcome and the probability of each outcome is written on the branch.

! **Tip**
Remember, for independent events
P(A and then B) = P(A) × P(B) and for mutually exclusive events
P(A or B) = P(A) + P(B).

Exercise 24.1

1 Anita has four cards. They are yellow, red, green and blue. She draws a card at random and then tosses a coin. Draw a tree diagram to show all possible outcomes.

2 The spinner shown has numbers on an inner circle and letters on an outer ring. When spun, it gives a result consisting of a number and a letter. Draw a tree diagram to show all possible outcomes when you spin it.

24.2 Calculating probability from tree diagrams and Venn diagrams

- To determine the probability of a combination of outcomes, multiply along each of the consecutive branches. If several combinations satisfy the same outcome conditions, then add the probabilities of the different paths.
- The sum of all the probabilities on a set of branches must equal one.

Exercise 24.2

1 When a coloured ball is drawn from a bag, a coin is tossed once or twice, depending on the colour of the ball drawn. There are three blue balls, two yellow balls and a black ball in the bag. The tree diagram shows the possible outcomes.

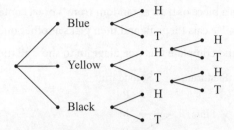

a Copy and label the diagram to show the probability of each event. Assume the draw of the balls is random and the coin is fair.

b Calculate the probability of a blue ball and a head.

c Calculate the probability of a yellow ball and two heads.

d Calculate the probability that you will not get heads at all.

2 The tree diagram below shows the possible outcomes when two coins are tossed.

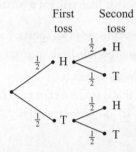

First toss   Second toss

a Copy and the tree diagram to show the possible outcomes when a third coin is tossed.

b Calculate the probability of tossing three heads.

c Calculate the probability of getting at least two tails.

d Calculate the probability of getting fewer heads than tails.

e Calculate the probability of getting an equal number of heads and tails.

3 When Zara drives to work she goes through a set of traffic lights and she passes a pedestrian crossing. She has worked out that the probability of the traffic lights being green is $\frac{3}{4}$ and the probability that she has to stop for a pedestrian is $\frac{2}{9}$.

a Draw a tree diagram to represent this situation.

b Calculate the probability that the traffic lights are not green when Zara gets to them and she has to stop at the pedestrian crossing.

c What is the probability that the light are green and she doesn't have to stop for a pedestrian?

4 Juan picks a piece of fruit at random from a bowl containing 5 plums, 7 mangos and 4 bananas. He eats the fruit and then picks another one at random.

  a Copy and complete this tree diagram to show all the probabilities.

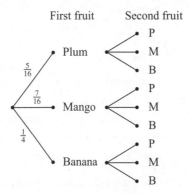

First fruit   Second fruit

Plum — P, M, B

Mango — P, M, B

Banana — P, M, B

$\frac{5}{16}$, $\frac{7}{16}$, $\frac{1}{4}$

  b Determine the probability that Juan will eat a banana first, followed by a plum.

5 A group of 75 students have a choice of two sports: basketball or swimming. 33 students play basketball and 47 swim. 24 students do both sports.

  a Represent this data on a Venn diagram.
  b Work out the probability that a student chosen at random from this group will:
    i do both sports   **ii** do neither sport   **iii** do at least one of the sports.

Mixed exercise

1 Dineo is playing a game where she rolls a normal six-sided die and tosses a coin. If the score on the die is even, she tosses the coin once. If the score on the die is odd, she tosses the coin twice.

  a Draw a tree diagram to show all possible outcomes.
  b Assuming the die and the coin are fair and all outcomes are equally likely, label the branches with the correct probabilities.
  c What is the probability of obtaining two tails?
  d What is the probability of obtaining a five, a head and a tail (in any order)?

2 Mrs Chan has a choice of ten mobile phone packages. Six of the packages offer free data bundles, five offer a free hands-free kit and three offer both.

  a Draw a Venn diagram to show this information.
  b Mrs Chan decides she is going to pick a package at random. Determine the probability of:
    i getting free data only
    ii getting free data and a hands-free kit
    iii getting free data or a hands-free kit.
  c Express her chances of getting neither as a percentage.

Answers

Chapter 1

Exercise 1.1

1 student's own tables

2 various answers possible; these are examples:
- **a** $12 > 11$
- **b** $\frac{3}{4} \leqslant 12$
- **c** $0.33 \approx \frac{1}{3}$
- **d** $4x = 12 \therefore x = 3$
- **e** $\sqrt{25} = 5$
- **f** $3^2 \neq 3 \times 2$
- **g** $(4+7) \geqslant (2+9)$
- **h** $4 < 5$

3
- **a** $-2, 0, -7, -32, \frac{1}{2}$
- **b** $\frac{1}{2}$
- **c** 3, 5, 23, 29
- **d** 1, 9, 4, 25

4
- **a** 121, 144, 169, 196, …
- **b** $\frac{1}{4}, \frac{1}{6}, \frac{2}{7}, \frac{2}{9}$, etc.
- **c** 83, 89, 97, 101, …
- **d** 2, 3, 5, 7

Exercise 1.2 A

1 **a** 18 **b** 36 **c** 90 **d** 24 **e** 36 **f** 24 **g** 72 **h** 96

2 **a** 6 **b** 18 **c** 9 **d** 3 **e** 10 **f** 1 **g** 12 **h** 50

Exercise 1.2 B

1 18 m

2 120 shoppers

3 20 students

4 14 cm, 165 squares

Exercise 1.3

1 **a** 2, 3, 5, 7 **b** 53, 59 **c** 97, 101, 103

2
- **a** $2 \times 2 \times 3 \times 3$
- **b** 5×13
- **c** $2 \times 2 \times 2 \times 2 \times 2 \times 2$
- **d** $2 \times 2 \times 3 \times 7$
- **e** $2 \times 2 \times 2 \times 2 \times 5$
- **f** $2 \times 2 \times 2 \times 5 \times 5 \times 5$
- **g** $2 \times 5 \times 127$
- **h** 13×151

3
- **a** LCM = 378, HCF = 1
- **b** LCM = 255, HCF = 5
- **c** LCM = 864, HCF = 3
- **d** LCM = 848, HCF = 1
- **e** LCM = 24264, HCF = 2
- **f** LCM = 2574, HCF = 6
- **g** LCM = 35200, HCF = 2
- **h** LCM = 17325, HCF = 5

Exercise 1.4

1 **a** 9 **b** 324 **c** 441 **d** 625 **e** 216 **f** 3375 **g** 5832 **h** 42875

2 **a** 11 **b** 8 **c** 21 **d** 11 **e** 36 **f** 51 **g** 56 **h** 27 **i** 6

3 square: 121, 144, 169, 196, 225, 256, 289
cube: 125, 216

4 square: 1, 49, 64, 256, 676, 625
cube: 1, 64

5 **a** 7 **b** 5 **c** 14 **d** 10 **e** 3 **f** 25 **g** $\frac{3}{4}$ **h** 5 **i** 2 **j** 5 **k** $1\frac{3}{4}$ **l** 12

6 **a** 64 **b** 2401 **c** 65536 **d** 1728 **e** 8000 **f** 100000 **g** 1954 **h** 155 **i** 1028 **j** 4096

Exercise 1.5

1 $-3\,°C$

2 **a** $-2\,°C$ **b** $-9\,°C$ **c** $-12\,°C$

3 **a** 4 **b** 7 **c** -1 **d** -2 **e** -3

Exercise 1.6

1 **a** 26 **b** 66 **c** 23.2 **d** 15.66
e 3.39 **f** 2.44 **g** 3.83 **h** 2.15 **i** 1.76 **j** 2.79 **k** 7.82 **l** 0.21 **m** 8.04 **n** 1.09 **o** 8.78 **p** 304.82 **q** 94.78 **r** 0.63 **s** 4.03 **t** 6.87 **u** 6.61 **v** 3.90 **w** -19.10 **x** 20.19

Exercise 1.7

1
- **a** 5.65 5.7 6
- **b** 9.88 9.9 10
- **c** 12.87 12.9 13
- **d** 0.01 0.0 0
- **e** 10.10 10.1 10
- **f** 45.44 45.4 45
- **g** 14.00 14.0 14
- **h** 26.00 26.0 26

2 **a** 53200 **b** 713000 **c** 17.4 **d** 0.00728

3 **a** 36 **b** 5.2 **c** 12000 **d** 0.0088 **e** 430000 **f** 120 **g** 0.0046 **h** 10

Mixed exercise

1 24, -12, 0, -15, -17

2 15, 30, 45, 60, 75

3 60

4 **a** $2 \times 2 \times 7 \times 7$ **b** $3 \times 3 \times 5 \times 41$ **c** $2 \times 2 \times 3 \times 3 \times 5 \times 7 \times 7$

5 14

6 **a** 5 **b** 5 **c** 64 **d** 145 **e** 138 **f** -168 **g** 5 **h** 10

7 **a** 16.07 **b** 9.79 **c** 13.51 **d** 11.01 **e** 0.73 **f** -7.74

8 **a** 1240 **b** 0.765 **c** 0.0238 **d** 31.5

9 Yes (80×80)

10 Yes, table sides are $\sqrt{1.4} = 1.18$ m or 118 cm long. Alternatively, area of cloth = 1.44 m² and this is greater than the table area.

11 1.5 m

Chapter 2

Exercise 2.1

1 a $7x$ b $x + 12$
   c $5x - 2$ d $2x - \dfrac{x}{3}$

2 a $p + 5$ b $p - 4$ c $4p$

3 a $\$\dfrac{x}{3}$

   b $\$\dfrac{x}{9}, \$\dfrac{2x}{9}, \$\dfrac{6x}{9}$ and $\$\dfrac{2x}{3}$

Exercise 2.2

1 a 20   b 60   c 11
   d 25   e −50   f 9
   g 75   h 100   i 9
   j 15   k 2   l 16
   m 15   n 3   o 15   p 7.5

2 a −10   b −10   c 12
   d −23   e −26   f 28
   g −1000   h 16000

3 a $54\,\text{cm}^2$ b $1.875\,\text{m}^2$
   c $110.25\,\text{cm}^2$ d $8\,\text{cm}^2$

Exercise 2.3

1 a $2m + 6n$
   b $6x + 2$
   c $a^2 + 6a - 5$
   d $y^2 - 5y - 2$
   e $3x^2 - 2x + 3$
   f $4x^2y - 2xy$
   g $5ab - 4ac$
   h $4x^2 + 5x - y - 5$

2 a $12xy$ b $8ab$
   c x^2 d $-6x$
   e $-30mn$ f $6x^2y$
   g $6xy^3$ h $-4x^3y$
   i $4b$ j $\dfrac{1}{4y}$
   k $3b$ l $\dfrac{9m}{4}$
   m $\dfrac{20y}{3x}$ n $\dfrac{3x^2}{y}$
   o $\dfrac{2y^2}{x^2}$ p $\dfrac{y^2}{2}$
   q $\dfrac{15a^2}{4}$ r $\dfrac{-14y}{5}$
   s $\dfrac{x}{6y}$ t $\dfrac{27x^2}{10}$

Exercise 2.4

1 a $3x + 6$ b $2x - 8$
   c $-2x - 6$ d $6x - 9$
   e $x^2 + 3x$ f $2x - x^2$
   g $-2x - 2x^2$ h $3x^2 - 9x$
   i $10x^2 - 4x$ j $-x + 2$
   k $4x^2 - 4xy$ l $-2x^2 + 4x$

2 a $2x^2 - 4x$ b $xy - 3x$
   c $-2x - 2$ d $-3x + 2$
   e $-2x^2 + 6x$ f $3x + 1$
   g $x^3 - 2x^2 - x$ h $x^2 + x + 2$

3 a $x^2 + \dfrac{x}{2}$ b $x^2 + xy$

   c $-8x^3 + 4x^2 + 2x$ d $\dfrac{x}{2} + \dfrac{3y}{2}$

   e $3x^2 - 6x$ f $-5x^2 - 6x$

Exercise 2.5 A

1 a x^{11} b y^{13}
   c $6x^3$ d $6x^8$
   e x^5y^4 f $48x^4$
   g $2x^3y^2$ h $-27x^{12}$

2 a $\dfrac{2x^2}{3}$ b $3x^2$

   c $\dfrac{2y}{3}$ d $\dfrac{x^{-1}}{2}$ or $\dfrac{1}{2x}$

   e $\dfrac{3x^{-2}y^{-5}}{2}$ or $\dfrac{3}{2x^2y^5}$

   f $2x^2y^{-3}z$ or $\dfrac{2x^2z}{y^3}$

   g $7x^{-1}$ or $\dfrac{7}{x}$

   h $4xy^{-1}$ or $\dfrac{4x}{y}$

   i $\dfrac{xy^{-1}}{3}$ or $\dfrac{x}{3y}$

   j x^3y^{-2} or $\dfrac{x^3}{y^2}$

   k $\dfrac{-3xz^3}{2}$ l $\dfrac{x^5}{2y^6}$

3 a $\dfrac{1}{3^2}$ or $\dfrac{1}{9}$

   b $\dfrac{3}{x^3}$

   c $\dfrac{x}{2y}$

   d $\dfrac{1}{xy}$

   e $\dfrac{1}{(8xy)^2}$ or $\dfrac{1}{64x^2y^2}$

f $16x^2y^2$ **g** y
h $\dfrac{x^3}{y^4}$ **i** $\dfrac{x^2}{y^2}$
j $\dfrac{y^2}{x^6}$ **k** $\dfrac{8x^7}{9y^3}$ **l** $\dfrac{4x^3}{7y^2}$

4 a x^6 b $-8x^9$
   c $16x^4$ d x^{27}
   e $-x^9y^{18}$ f $x^{12}y^8$
   g $-2x^3y^3$ h $16x^5$
   i 1 j $x^{16}y^4$
   k $3^y x^{y^2}$ l $-8x^6$

Exercise 2.5 B

1 a $\dfrac{x^6}{y^2}$ b $3x^4y$

   c $\dfrac{2x^2}{3y}$ d xy^{10}

   e $\dfrac{5x^9}{2y^3}$ f x^7y^3

   g $\dfrac{50x^3}{27y}$ h $\dfrac{49}{25x^3y}$

   i x^7y j $\dfrac{8x^{10}y^3}{3}$

   k $\dfrac{x^{16}}{y^{16}}$ l $\dfrac{3125x^4y^2}{16}$

2 a $\dfrac{x^8}{y^2}$ b $\dfrac{x^5}{y^4}$

   c $\dfrac{8}{x^5y^7}$ d $\dfrac{1}{x^9}$

   e $\dfrac{y^{16}}{x^{22}}$ f $\dfrac{y^{22}}{2x^4}$

3 a $x^{\frac{1}{2}}$ b $x^{\frac{8}{15}}$

   c $x^{\frac{1}{6}}$ d $x^{\frac{1}{9}}$

   e $8x^3$ f $2x^3y^{\frac{1}{3}}$

   g $x^{\frac{1}{2}}y^4$ h x^3y^{-1} or $\dfrac{x^3}{y}$

   i x^3 j $x^{-2}y^{-4}$ or $\dfrac{1}{x^2y^4}$

   k y^{-2} or $\dfrac{1}{y^2}$

Mixed exercise

1 a $x + 12$ b $x - 4$
   c $5x$ d $\dfrac{x}{3}$

e $4x$ **f** $\frac{x}{4}$

g $12 - x$ **h** $x^3 - x$

2 a -6 **b** 24 **c** $\frac{-14}{9}$

3 a -2 **b** $\frac{2}{3}$ **c** 5

d 7 **e** -2

4 a 630 **b** 44

c 150 **d** 12

5 a $2y + 10$ **b** $4y - 4$

c $6x + 15$ **d** $12x - 8y$

e $xy + 2x$ **f** $20x - 14y + 6z$

g $6x^2 + 2x$ **h** $2x + 7$

i $4x + 18$ **j** $15x - 6y$

6 a $9a + b$

b $x^2 + 3x - 2$

c $-4a^4b + 6a^2b^3$

d $-7x + 4$

e $\frac{4x}{y}$

f $5x - \frac{5y}{2}$

7 a $11x - 3$

b $6x^2 + 15x - 8$

c $-2x^2 + 5x + 12$

d $-x^3 + 3x^2 - x + 5$

8 a $\frac{5x^5}{6}$ **b** 15

c $\frac{1}{x^4}$ **d** $16x^4y^8$

e $\frac{64x^9}{y^{15}}$ **f** x^9y^8

g $\frac{9x^4}{4y^3}$ **h** $\frac{xy^6}{2}$

9 a 2 **b** -10

c 2 **d** $\frac{3}{2}$

Chapter 3
Exercise 3.1 A

1 a obtuse, 112°   **b** acute, 32°

c right, 90°   **d** reflex, 279°

e obtuse, 125°   **f** reflex, 193°

2 a i 90°   **ii** 180°

b 30°

c 360°

d quarter to one or 12:45

3 No. If the acute angle is $\leqslant$ 45° it will produce an acute or right angle.

4 Yes. The smallest obtuse angle is 91° and the largest is 179°. Half of those will range from 45.5° to 89.5°, all of which are acute.

5 a 45°   **b** 28°

c $(90 - x)°$ **d** $x°$

6 a 135°   **b** 90°

c 76°   **d** $(180 - x)°$

e $x°$ **f** $(90 + x)°$

g $(90 - x)°$ **h** $220 - 2x$

Exercise 3.1 B

1 $z = 65°$ (angles on line); $y = 65°$ (VO); $x = 25$ (comp angle to z)

2 angle $QON = 48°$, so $a = 48°$ (VO)

3 a angle $EOD = 41°$ (angles on line), so $x = 41°$ (VO)

b $x = 20°$ (angles round point)

Exercise 3.1 C

1 angle $HGB = 143°$ (angles on line); angle $AGF = 143°$ (VO); angle $BGF = 37°$ (VO); angle $DFG = 143°$ (corr angles); angle $CFG = 37°$ (corr angles); angle $CFE = 143°$ (VO); angle $EFD = 37°$ (VO)

2 a $x = 68°$ (angle $BFG = 68°$, angles on line, then alt angles)

b $x = 85°$ (co-int angles); $y = 72°$ (alt angles)

c $x = 99°$ (co-int angles); $y = 123°$ (angle $ABF = 123°$, co-int angles then VO)

d $x = 47°$ (alt angles); $y = 81°$ (angles in triangle BEF or on st line); $z = 52°$ (alt angles)

e $x = 72°$ (angle $BFE = 72°$, then alt angles); $y = 43°$ (angles in triangle BCJ)

f $x = 45°$ (angles round a point); $y = 90°$ (co-int angles)

3 a $x = 15°$ (co-int angles)

b $x = 60°$ (co-int angles)

c $x = 45°$ (angle STQ corr angles then VO)

d $x = 77.5°$ and $y = 75°$ (co-int angles)

e $x = 90°$ (angle ECD and angle ACD co-int angles then angles round as point)

f $x = 18°$ (angle DFE co-int with angle CDF then angle BFE co-int with angle ABF)

Exercise 3.2

1 a 74° (angles in triangle)

b 103° (angles in triangle)

c 58° (ext angle equals sum int opps)

d 51° (ext angle equals sum int opps)

e 21° (ext angle equals sum int opps)

f 68° (ext angle equals sum int opps)

g 53° (base angles isosceles)

h 60° (equilateral triangle)

i $x = 58°$ (base angles isosceles and angles in triangle); $y = 26°$ (ext angles equals sum int opps)

j $x = 33°$ (base angles isosceles then ext angles equals sum int opps)

k $x = 45°$ (co-int angles then angles in triangle)

l $x = 45°$ (base angles isosceles); $y = 75°$ (base angles isosceles)

2 a $x = 36$; so $A = 36°$ and $B = 72°$

b $x = 40$; so $A = 80°$; $B = 40°$ and angle $ACD = 120°$

c $x = 60°$

d $x = 72°$

e $x = 60°$; so $R = 60°$ and angle $RTS = 120°$

f $x = 110°$

Exercise 3.3

1 a square, rhombus

b rectangle, square

c square, rectangle

d square, rectangle, rhombus, parallelogram

e square, rectangle

f square, rectangle, parallelogram, rhombus

g square, rhombus, kite

h rhombus, square, kite

i rhombus, square, kite

2 a $x = 69°$

b $x = 64°$

c $x = 52°$

d $x = 115°$

e $x = 30°$; $2x = 60°$; $3x = 90°$

f $a = 44°$; $b = 68°$; $c = d = 68°$; $e = 44°$

Exercise 3.4

1 a 60°   **b** 720°   **c** 120°

2 a 1080°   **b** 1440°   **c** 2340°

3 $\frac{900}{7} = 128.57°$

4 20 sides

5 a 165.6   **b** $\frac{360}{14.4} = 25$ sides

Exercise 3.5

Diagram	Name	Definition
	circumference	distance round the outside of a circle
	diameter	distance across a circle through centre
	radius	distance from centre to circumference; half a diameter
	arc	part of the circumference of a circle
	chord	line joining any two points on the circumference
	semi-circle	half a circle
	segment	piece of circle created by chord
	sector	slice of circle; area between two radii
	tangent	line that touches a circle at one point only

Exercise 3.6

1 a Either B A D E C or B D A E C

  b You can start with any of the sides and draw the arcs in different order.

2 student's own diagram

3 student's own diagram

4 scalene

5 a He's drawn the arcs using the length of *AC* instead of the lengths of the other two given sides.

  b

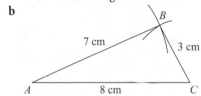

Mixed exercise

1 a when two parallel lines are cut by a transversal, the alternate angles are formed inside the parallel lines, on opposite sides of the transversal

  b a triangle with two equal sides

  c a quadrilateral with two pairs of adjacent sides equal in length

  d a quadrilateral with four equal sides and opposite sides parallel to each other

  e a many-sided shape with all sides equal and all interior angles equal

  f an eight-sided shape

2 a $x = 113°$

  b $x = 41°$

  c $x = 89°$

  d $x = 66°$

  e $x = 74°; y = 106°; z = 46°$

  f $x = 38°; y = 104°$

  g $x = 110°; y = 124°$

  h $x = 40°; y = 70°; z = 70°$

3 a $x = 60 + 60 + 120 = 240°$

  b $x = 90 + 90 + 135 = 315°$

4 a i radius   **ii** chord

    iii diameter

  b *AO, DO, OC, OB*

  c 24.8 cm

  d student's own diagram

5 student's own diagram

6 a In the diagram, *AC* and *BC* are radii of the circles, so they must measure half the diameter, in other words, 4.5 cm long. Use that measurement to construct the equilateral triangle.

  b

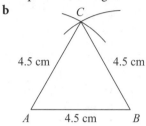

Chapter 4

Exercise 4.1

1 a gender, eye colour, hair colour

  b height, shoe size, mass, number of brothers/sisters

  c shoe size, number of brothers/ sisters

  d height, mass

  e possible answers include: gender, eye colour, hair colour – observation; height, mass – measured; shoe size, number of siblings – survey, questionnaire

Exercise 4.2

1

Mark	Tally	Frequency
1	/	1
2	//	2
3	//	2
4	LH1	5
5	LH1 ////	9
6	LH1 //	7
7	LH1 /	6
8	///	3
9	///	3
10	//	2

2 a

Score	1	2	3	4	5	6
Frequency	5	8	7	7	7	6

b The scores are fairly similar for even a low number of throws, so the dice is probably fair.

3 a

Score	Frequency
0–29	1
30–39	1
40–49	7
50–59	19
60–69	12
70–79	6
80–100	4

b 10   **c** 2   **d** 26

e There are very few marks at the low and high end of the scale.

f

Stem	Leaf
2	6
3	8
4	0 2 4 5 6 8 9
5	1 2 3 4 4 4 4 5 5 5 5 6 6 7 7 7 8 9 9
6	0 1 3 3 3 5 5 7 7 7 7 9 9
7	0 1 3 6 8 8
8	0 2 8
9	1

Key: 2 | 6 = 26 percent

The actual data values are given, so you can calculate exact mode, median and range. You can also see the shape of the distribution of the data quite clearly.

4 a

Eye colour	Brown	Blue	Green
Male	4	0	1
Female	2	2	1

b

Hair colour	Brown	Black	Blonde
Male	2	2	1
Female	1	4	0

No. of brothers/sisters	0	1	2	3	4
Male	0	1	1	2	1
Female	2	1	1	1	0

c student's own sentences

5 a

Stem	Leaf
0	1 2 5 7
1	2 2 6 8 9
2	0 3 4 9
3	1 1 1 3 5 7 9
4	1 3 8
5	1

Key: 0 | 1 = 1 car, 1 | 2 = 12 cars

b 51 cars

Exercise 4.3

1 a pictogram
b number of students in each year group in a school
c 30 students
d half a stick figure
e 225
f Year 11; 285
g rounded; unlikely the year groups will all be multiples of 15

2 student's own chart

3 a number of boys and girls in class 10A
b 18   **c** 30
d the favourite sports of students in 10A, separated by gender
e athletics
f athletics
g 9

4 a student's own chart
b student's own chart

5 a cars   **b** 17%   **c** 11
d handcarts and bicycles

6 a student's own chart
b 6   **c** 50   **d** C

Mixed exercise

1 a survey or questionnaire
b discrete; you cannot have half a child
c quantitative; it can be counted
d

No. of children in family	0	1	2	3	4	5	6
Frequency	7	10	11	12	5	2	1

e student's own chart
f student's own chart

2 a

Boys Leaf	Stem	Girls Leaf
	14	5 7
9	15	4 7 9
7 6 6 5	16	1 2 2 3 4 4 6
8 8 6 5 5 4	17	1 1
7 5 4 3	18	0

Key: 9 | 15 = 159 cm and 14 | 5 = 145 cm

b 13
c The boys' measurements are clustered more towards the higher end, suggesting they are taller (as a group) than the girls in this class.

3 student's own pictogram

4 a compound bar chart
b It shows how many people, out of every 100, have a mobile phone and how many have a land line phone.
c No. The figures are percentages.
d Canada, USA and Denmark
e Germany, UK, Sweden and Italy
f Denmark
g own opinion with reason

Chapter 5
Exercise 5.1

1 a $\frac{1}{2}$ **b** $\frac{1}{3}$ **c** $\frac{1}{3}$

d $\frac{1}{4}$ **e** $\frac{1}{4}$ **f** $\frac{1}{8}$

g $\frac{1}{5}$ **h** $\frac{2}{3}$ **i** $\frac{3}{4}$ **j** $\frac{3}{8}$

2 a 33   **b** 300   **c** 25
d 65   **e** 168   **f** 55
g 117   **h** 48   **i** 104   **j** 63

Exercise 5.2

1 a $\frac{13}{6}$ **b** $\frac{25}{8}$ **c** $\frac{17}{11}$

d $\frac{93}{10}$ **e** $\frac{59}{5}$ **f** $\frac{15}{4}$

g $\frac{59}{4}$ **h** $\frac{25}{9}$ **i** $\frac{28}{3}$ **j** $\frac{-25}{9}$

2 a $\frac{1}{25}$ **b** $\frac{1}{10}$ **c** $\frac{2}{5}$

d $\frac{9}{20}$ **e** $\frac{16}{99}$ **f** $\frac{4}{11}$

g $\frac{30}{91}$ h $\frac{6}{25}$ i $\frac{15}{28}$ j $\frac{9}{44}$

3 a $\frac{108}{5}$ b $\frac{63}{13}$ c 14

d $\frac{28}{5}$ e 3   f $\frac{6}{19}$

g 120   h $\frac{3}{14}$ i 72

j 3   k $\frac{233}{50}$ l $\frac{7}{4}$

4 a $\frac{11}{20}$ b $\frac{11}{30}$ c $\frac{4}{45}$

d $\frac{13}{24}$ e $\frac{4}{15}$ f $\frac{19}{60}$

g $\frac{19}{21}$ h $\frac{16}{15}$ i $\frac{13}{24}$

j $\frac{35}{6}$ k $\frac{183}{56}$ l $\frac{161}{20}$

m $\frac{18}{65}$ n $\frac{41}{40}$ o $\frac{29}{21}$

p $\frac{-5}{6}$ q $\frac{-10}{3}$ r $\frac{-26}{9}$

s $\frac{13}{21}$ t $\frac{43}{12}$

5 a 24   b $\frac{96}{7}$ c $\frac{7}{96}$

d $\frac{10}{27}$ e $\frac{10}{9}$ f $\frac{9}{14}$

6 a $\frac{38}{9}$ b $\frac{4}{5}$ c $\frac{39}{7}$

d $\frac{19}{4}$ e $\frac{5}{12}$ f $\frac{215}{72}$

g 0   h $\frac{11}{170}$ i $\frac{187}{9}$

7 a $525   b $375

8 a 300
   b 450 per day $\times$ 5 days = 2250 tiles per week

Exercise 5.3 A

1 a 50%   b 67%   c 16.7%
   d 62.5%   e 29.8%   f 30%
   g 4%   h 47%   i 112%
   j 207%

2 a $\frac{1}{4}$ b $\frac{4}{5}$ c $\frac{9}{10}$

d $\frac{1}{8}$ e $\frac{1}{2}$ f $\frac{49}{50}$

g $\frac{3}{5}$ h $\frac{11}{50}$

3 a 60 kg   b $24
   c 150 litres   d 55 ml
   e $64   f $19.5
   g 18 km   h 0.2 grams
   i $2.08   j 47.5
   k $2   l 4.2 kg

4 a +20%   b −10%
   c +53.3%   d +3.3%
   e −28.3%   f +33.3%
   g +2566.7%

5 a $54.72   b $945
   c $32.28   d $40236
   e $98.55   f $99.68

6 a $58.48   b $520
   c $83.16   d $19882
   e $76.93   f $45.24

Exercise 5.3 B

1 28595 tickets

2 1800 shares

3 $129375

4 21.95%

5 $15696

6 $6228

7 2.5 grams

8 $\frac{7}{25}$ = 28% increase, so $7 more is better

Exercise 5.4 A

1 a 4.5×10^4 b 8×10^5
   c 8×10 d 2.345×10^6
   e 4.19×10^6 f 3.2×10^{10}
   g 6.5×10^{-3} h 9×10^{-3}
   i 4.5×10^{-4} j 8×10^{-7}
   k 6.75×10^{-3} l 4.5×10^{-10}

2 a 2500   b 39000
   c 426500   d 0.00001045
   e 0.00000915   f 0.000000001
   g 0.000028   h 94000000
   i 0.00245

Exercise 5.4 B

1 a 5.62×10^{21} b 6.56×10^{-17}
   c 1.28×10^{-14} d 1.44×10^{13}
   e 1.58×10^{-20} f 5.04×10^{18}
   g 1.98×10^{12} h 1.52×10^{17}
   i 2.29×10^8

2 a 12×10^{30}
   b 4.5×10^{11}
   c 3.375×10^{36}
   d 1.32×10^{-11}
   e 2×10^{26}
   f 2.67×10^5
   g 1.2×10^2
   h 2×10^{-3}
   i 2.09×10^{-8}

3 a the Sun   b 6.051×10^6

4 a 500 seconds = 5×10^2 seconds
   b 19166.67 seconds = 1.92×10^4 seconds

Exercise 5.5

1 a $4 \times 5 = 20$ b $70 \times 5 = 350$
   c $1000 \times 7 = 7000$
   d $42 \div 6 = 7$

2 a 20   b 3
   c 12   d 243

Mixed exercise

1 a 40   b 6
   c 22   d 72

2 a $\frac{4}{5}$ b $\frac{2}{3}$ c $\frac{2}{3}$

3 a $\frac{1}{6}$ b 63   c $\frac{5}{3}$

d $\frac{13}{15}$ e $\frac{3}{44}$ f $\frac{31}{48}$

g $\frac{71}{6}$ h $\frac{361}{16}$ i $\frac{334}{45}$

4 $\frac{1}{4}$

5 a 8%   b 5%   c 63.33%

6 2.67%

7 a 24.6 kg   b 0.5 l   c $70

8 a 12.5%   b 33.33%   c 34%

9 $103.50

10 $37.40

11 67.9%

12 2940 m

13 a $760   b $40000

14 a 5.9×10^9 km
   b 5.753×10^9 km

Chapter 6

Exercise 6.1

1 a $-2x-2y$ **b** $-5a+5b$
   c $6x-3y$ **d** $8x-4xy$
   e $-2x^2-6xy$ **f** $-9x+9$
   g $12-6a$ **h** $3-4x-y$
   i 3 **j** $-3x-7$
   k $2x^2-2xy$ **l** $-3x^2+6xy$

2 a $14x-2y-9x$
   b $-5xy+10x$
   c $6x-6y-2xy$
   d $-2x-5y-2xy$
   e $12xy-14-y+3x$
   f $4x^2-2x^2y-3y$
   g $-2x^2+2x+5$
   h $6x^2+4y-8xy$
   i $-\frac{1}{2}(8x-2)+3-(x+7)$

Exercise 6.2

1 a $x=16$ **b** $x=24$
   c $x=8$ **d** $x=54$
   e $x=7$ **f** $x=-2$
   g $x=-16$ **h** $x=-60$
   i $x=-9$ **j** $x=-15$
   k $x=13$ **l** $x=15$

2 a $x=8$ **b** $x=15$
   c $x=-\frac{5}{2}=-2\frac{1}{2}$ **d** $x=-10$
   e $x=-4$ **f** $x=-12$

3 a $x=3$ **b** $x=4$
   c $x=\frac{9}{2}=4\frac{1}{2}$ **d** $x=4$
   e $x=\frac{36}{10}=\frac{18}{5}=3\frac{3}{5}$ **f** $x=5$
   g $x=2$ **h** $x=-5$
   i $x=4$ **j** $x=-\frac{3}{2}=-1\frac{1}{2}$
   k $x=\frac{11}{2}=5\frac{1}{2}$ **l** $x=3$

4 a $x=10$ **b** $x=-2$
   c $x=-\frac{8}{3}=-2\frac{2}{3}$ **d** $x=\frac{4}{3}=1\frac{1}{3}$
   e $x=8$ **f** $x=\frac{1}{4}$
   g $x=-4$ **h** $x=-9$
   i $x=-10$ **j** $x=-13$
   k $x=-34$ **l** $x=\frac{20}{13}=1\frac{7}{13}$

5 a $x=18$ **b** $x=27$
   c $x=24$ **d** $x=-44$
   e $x=17$ **f** $x=29$
   g $x=11$ **h** $x=\frac{23}{6}=3\frac{5}{6}$
   i $x=-1$ **j** $x=\frac{9}{2}=4\frac{1}{2}$
   k $x=-\frac{1}{3}$ **l** $x=9$
   m $x=\frac{16}{13}=1\frac{3}{13}$ **n** $x=10$
   o $x=42$ **p** $x=\frac{-4}{11}$

Exercise 6.3

1 a 3 **b** 8 **c** 5
   d a **e** $3y$ **f** $5ab$
   g $4xy$ **h** pq **i** $7ab$
   j xy^2z **k** ab^3 **l** $3xy$

2 a $12(x+4)$ **b** $2(1+4y)$
   c $4(a-4)$ **d** $2(x-6)$
   e $4(x-5)$ **f** $8(2a-1)$
   g $x(3-y)$ **h** $a(b+5)$
   i $3(x-5y)$ **j** $8(a+3)$
   k $6(2x-3)$ **l** $8xz(3y-1)$
   m $3b(3a-4c)$ **n** $2y(3x-7z)$
   o $2x(7-13y)$ **p** $-14x^2-7x^5$

3 a $x(x+8)$ **b** $a(12-a)$
   c $x(9x+4)$ **d** $2x(11-8x)$
   e $2b(3ab+4)$ **f** $18xy(1-2x)$
   g $3x(2-3x)$ **h** $2xy^2(7x-3)$
   i $3abc^2(3c-ab)$ **j** $x(4x-7y)$
   k $b^2(3a-4c)$ **l** $7ab(2a-3b)$

4 a $(3+y)(x+4)$
   b $(y-3)(x+5)$
   c $(a+2b)(3-2a)$
   d $(2a-b)(4a-3)$
   e $(2-y)(x+1)$
   f $(x-3)(x+4)$
   g $(2+y)(9-x)$
   h $(2b-c)(4a+1)$
   i $(x-6)(3x-5)$
   j $(x-y)(x-2)$
   k $(2x+3)(3x+y)$
   l $(x-y)(4-3x)$

Exercise 6.4 A

1 $m=\frac{D}{k}$

2 $c=y-mx$

3 $b=\frac{P+c}{a}$

4 $b=\frac{a-c}{x}$

5 a $a=c-b$ **b** $a=2c+3b$
   c $a=\frac{c+d}{b}$ **d** $a=\frac{d-c}{b}$
   e $a=bc-d$ (or $a=-d+bc$)
   f $a=d+bc$ **g** $a=\frac{cd-b}{2}$
   h $a=\frac{de-c}{b}$ **i** $a=\frac{e+d}{bc}$
   j $a=\frac{ef-d}{bc}$ **k** $a=\frac{c(f-de)}{b}$
   l $a=\frac{d(e-c)}{b}$ **m** $a=\frac{d}{c}+b$
   n $a=\frac{d}{c}-2b$

Exercise 6.4 B

1 a $b=\frac{P}{2}-l$ **b** $b=35.5\,\text{cm}$

2 a $r=\frac{C}{2\pi}$ **b** $9\,\text{cm}$ **c** $46\,\text{cm}$

3 use $b=\frac{2A}{h}-a$; $b=3.8\,\text{cm}$

Mixed exercise

1 a $x=-3$ **b** $x=-6$
   c $x=9$ **d** $x=-6$
   e $x=2$ **f** $x=-13$
   g $x=1.5$ **h** $x=\frac{15}{7}=2\frac{1}{7}$

2 a $x=\frac{m+r}{np}$ **b** $x=\frac{mq-p}{n}$

3 a $3x+2$ **b** $-12x^2+8x$
   c $-8x+4y-6$ **d** $-16y+2y^2$
   e $11x+5$ **f** $5x^2+7x-4$
   g $-2x^2+11x$ **h** $10x^2+24x$

4 a $4(x-2)$ **b** $3(4x-y)$
   c $-2(x+2)$ **d** $3x(y-8)$
   e $7xy(2xy+1)$ **f** $(x-y)(2+x)$
   g $(4+3x)(x-3)$
   h $4x(x+y)(x-2)$

5 a $4(x-7)=4x-28$
   b $2x(x+9)=2x^2+18x$
   c $4x(4x+3y)=16x^2+12xy$
   d $19x(x+2y)=19x^2+38xy$

Chapter 7

Exercise 7.1 A

1 a 120 mm   **b** 45 cm
   c 128 mm   **d** 98 mm
   e 40 cm   **f** 233 mm

2 a 15.71 m   **b** 43.98 cm
   c 53.99 mm   **d** 21.57 m
   e 18.85 m   **f** 150.80 mm
   g 24.38 m

3 90 m

4 $164 \times 45.50 = \$7462$

5 9 cm each

6 about 88 cm

7 a 63π cm   **b** 70π cm

Exercise 7.1 B

1 a 841 mm²   **b** 406 m²
   c 224 cm²   **d** 1.53 m²
   e 372 cm²   **f** 399 cm²
   g 150 cm²   **h** 42 cm²
   i 58.5 cm²   **j** 2193.5 mm²
   k 5.76 m²   **l** 7261.92 cm²
   m 243 cm²

2 a 7853.98 mm²   **b** 2290.22 cm²
   c 7696.90 mm²   **d** 18.10 m²
   e 17.45 cm²

3 a 288 cm²   **b** 82 cm²
   c 373.5 cm²   **d** 581.5 cm²
   e 366 cm²   **f** 39 cm²
   g 272.97 cm²   **h** 4000 cm²
   i 5640.43 cm²

4 a 30 cm²   **b** 90 cm²
   c 36.4 cm²   **d** 61.2 cm²
   e 720 cm²   **f** 600 +
                         625π cm²

5 11.1 m²

6 70 mm = 7 cm

Exercise 7.1 C

1 a 43.98 mm   **b** 47.12 cm
   c 8.38 mm

2 6 671.70 km

3 a 24π cm²   **b** 233.33π cm²
   c $(81\pi - 162)$ mm²

4 61.4 cm²

Exercise 7.2

1 a cube
   b cuboid
   c square-based pyramid
   d octahedron

2 a cuboid
   b triangular prism
   c cylinder

3 The following are examples; there are other possible nets.

a

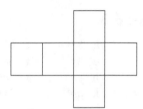

b

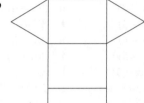

c

d

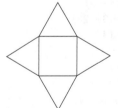

Exercise 7.3

1 a 2.56 m²   **b** 523.2 m²
   c 13.5 cm²   **d** 402.12 mm²

2 a 384 cm²   **b** 8 cm

3 a 340 cm²   **b** 153000 cm²
   c 4 tins

4 a 90000 mm³   **b** 60 cm³
   c 20420.35 mm³   **d** 1120 cm³

   e 960 cm³   **f** 5.76 m³
   g 1800 cm³   **h** 1.95 m³

5 a 5.28 cm³   **b** 33510.32 m³
   c 25.2 cm³

6 332.5 cm³

7 a 225 m³   **b** 44

8 67.5π m³

9 various answers – for example:

Volume (mm³)	64000	64000	64000	64000
Length (mm)	80	50	100	50
Breadth (mm)	40	64	80	80
Height (mm)	20	20	8	16

Mixed exercise

1 a 346 cm²   **b** 66.0 cm

2 4.55 cm

3 a 2000 mm²   **b** 33000 mm²
   c 35 cm²   **d** 80 cm²
   e 106 cm²   **f** 35 cm²
   g 175.93 m

4 15 m

5 a cuboid is smaller
   b 14265.48 mm³
   c student's own diagram
   d cylinder 7539.82 mm², cuboid 9000 mm²

6 64

Chapter 8

Exercise 8.1

1 a red $= \frac{3}{10}$, white $= \frac{9}{25}$, green $= \frac{17}{50}$

   b 30%   **c** 1   **d** $\frac{1}{3}$

2 a 0.61, 0.22, 0.11, 0.05, 0.01
   b **i** highly likely
       ii unlikely
       iii highly unlikely

Exercise 8.2

1 a red, blue   **b** $\frac{1}{2}$ **c** yes

2 a 1, 2, 3, 4, 5 or 6

   b $\frac{1}{2}$ **c** $\frac{1}{2}$ **d** 0

3 a 1, 2, 3, 4, 5, 6, 7, 8, 9, or 10

 b i $\frac{1}{10} = 0.1$ **ii** 1 **iii** $\frac{3}{10}$

 iv $\frac{3}{10}$ **v** $\frac{2}{5}$ **vi** $\frac{1}{2}$

 vii $\frac{3}{10}$ **viii** $\frac{9}{10}$ **ix** 0

4 a $\frac{2}{5}$ **b** no sugar; probability $= \frac{3}{5}$

5 a 0 **b** $\frac{1}{4}$ **c** $\frac{1}{2}$

6 a $\frac{1}{3}$ or 0.33 **b** $\frac{1}{2}$ or 0.5

 c $\frac{1}{7}$ or 0.14

7 a $\frac{7}{20}$ **b** $\frac{1}{2}$ **c** $\frac{2}{5}$

 d $\frac{3}{10}$ **e** $\frac{1}{5}$

8 $\frac{13}{40}$

Exercise 8.3

1 0.73

2 $\frac{5}{8}$

3 a 0.16 **b** 0.84 **c** 0.6
 d strawberry 63, lime 66, lemon 54, blackberry 69, apple 48

4 a 0.12 **b** 0.88 **c** 0.24
 d 2000

Exercise 8.4

1

	H	T
H	HH	HT
T	TH	TT

 a $\frac{3}{4}$ **b** $\frac{1}{4}$

2 a

		Yellow	
	1	**2**	**3**
1	1, 1	1, 2	1, 3
Green **2**	2, 1	2, 2	2, 3
3	3, 1	3, 2	3, 3

 b 9 **c** $\frac{1}{3}$ **d** $\frac{1}{3}$

3 a $\frac{1}{36}$ **b** $\frac{1}{18}$

 c $\frac{1}{6}$ **d** $\frac{1}{9}$

Exercise 8.5

1 a

	A	U	A
C	CA	CU	CA
L	LA	LU	LA
C	CA	CU	CA
T	TA	TU	TA
T	TA	TU	TA

 b $\frac{4}{15}$ **c** $\frac{1}{5}$ **d** $\frac{4}{15}$

2 $\frac{1}{6}$

3 a $\frac{16}{81}$ **b** $\frac{25}{81}$ **c** $\frac{40}{81}$

Mixed exercise

1 a 10 000 **b** 0.4083
 c 0.5917 **c** $\frac{1}{2}$

 d could be – probability of the tails outcome is higher than the heads outcome for a great many tosses

2 a $\frac{1}{2}$ **b** $\frac{2}{5}$ **c** $\frac{1}{10}$

 d 0 **e** $\frac{9}{10}$ **f** $\frac{9}{10}$

 g $\frac{1}{2}$

3 a $\frac{1}{36}$ **b** $7, \frac{1}{6}$

 c $\frac{1}{2}$ **d** $\frac{1}{6}$

4 a $\frac{1}{10}$ **b** $\frac{1}{2}$ **c** $\frac{1}{5}$

5 a $\frac{1}{6}$ **b** $\frac{1}{3}$

 c 0 **d** $\frac{1}{2}$

Chapter 9

Exercise 9.1

1 a 17, 19, 21 (add 2)
 b 121, 132, 143 (add 11)
 c 8, 4, 2 (divide by 2)
 d 40, 48, 56 (add 8)
 e −10, −12, −14 (subtract 2)
 f 2, 4, 8 (multiply by 2)
 g 11, 16, 22 (add one more each time than added to previous term)
 h 21, 26, 31 (add 5)

2 a 7, 9, 11, 13 **b** 37, 32, 27, 22
 c $1, \frac{1}{2}, \frac{1}{4}, \frac{1}{8}$ **d** 5, 11, 23, 47
 e 100, 47, 20.5, 7.25

3 a 5, 7, 9 $T_{35} = 73$
 b 1, 4, 9 $T_{35} = 1225$
 c 5, 11, 17 $T_{35} = 209$
 d 0, 7, 26 $T_{35} = 42874$
 e 0, 2, 6 $T_{35} = 1190$
 f 1, −1, −3 $T_{35} = -67$

4 a $8n - 6$ **b** 1594 **c** 30th
 d $T_{18} = 138$ and $T_{19} = 146$, so 139 is not a term

5 a $2n + 5$ $T_{50} = 105$
 b $3 - 8n$ $T_{50} = -397$
 c $6n - 4$ $T_{50} = 296$
 d n^2 $T_{50} = 2500$
 e $1.2n + 1.1$ $T_{50} = 61.1$

Exercise 9.2

1 a $\sqrt[3]{16}, \sqrt{12}, 0.090090009\ldots$

 b $\sqrt{45}, \sqrt[3]{90}, \pi, \sqrt{8}$

Exercise 9.3 A

1 a false **b** true **c** false
 d true **e** false

2 a {}
 b {1, 3, 5, 6, 7, 9, 11, 12, 13, 15, 18}

3 a {−2, −1, 0, 1, 2}
 b {1, 2, 3, 4, 5}

4 a $A \cup B = $ {1, 2, 3, 4, 5, 6, 7, 8, 9}
 b $A \cap B = $ {}

Exercise 9.3 B

1

2 a 9
 b 20
 c {c, h, i, s, y}
 d {c, e, h, i, m, p, r, s, t, y}

3 a

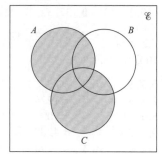

b

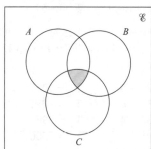

4

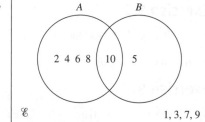

a $A \cap B = \{10\}$ **b** 4
c $A \cup B = \{2, 4, 5, 6, 8, 10\}$

5

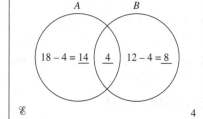

6 a

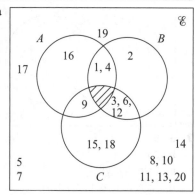

b i $A \cap B \cap C = \{\}$
   ii $A \cup B \cup C = \{1, 2, 3, 4, 6, 9,$
      $12, 15, 18\}$
   iii $D = \{5, 7, 8, 10, 11, 13, 14, 17,$
      $19, 20\}$

7

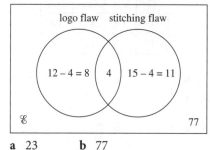

T-shirts tested (100)

a 23   **b** 77

Mixed exercise

1 a $5n - 4$ $T_{120} = 596$
   b $26 - 6n$ $T_{120} = -694$
   c $3n - 1$ $T_{120} = 359$

2 $0.213231234\ldots, \sqrt{2}, 4\pi$

3 a $\frac{2}{3}, \frac{3}{5}, -4, 0, 25, 3.21, -2.5, 85, 0.75$

   b $-4, 0, 25, 85$

4 a

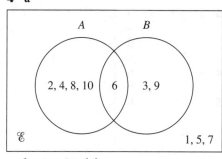

b $A \cap B = \{6\}$
c $n(A \cup B) = 7$

5

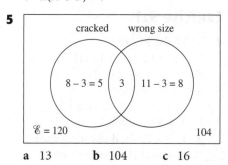

a 13   **b** 104   **c** 16

Chapter 10
Exercise 10.1

1 a

x	−1	0	1	2	3
y	4	5	6	7	8

b

x	−1	0	1	2	3
y	1	−1	−3	−5	−7

c

x	−1	0	1	2	3
y	9	7	5	3	1

d

x	−1	0	1	2	3
y	−1	−2	−3	−4	−5

e

x	4	4	4	4	4
y	−1	0	1	2	3

(in fact, any five values of y are correct)

f

x	−1	0	1	2	3
y	−2	−2	−2	−2	−2

g

x	−1	0	1	2	3
y	1.5	−0.5	−2.5	−4.5	−6.5

h

x	−1	0	1	2	3
y	−1.2	−0.8	−0.4	0	0.4

i

x	−1	0	1	2	3
y	−1	−0.5	0	0.5	1

j

x	−1	0	1	2	3
y	0.5	−0.5	−1.5	−2.5	−3.5

2 student's graphs of values above

3 $y = x - 2$

4 a no   **b** yes   **c** yes
   d no   **e** no   **f** no
   g yes (horizontal lines)
   h yes (vertical lines)

5 a $m = 1$ **b** $m = -1$
   c $m = -1$ **d** $m = \frac{6}{7}$
   e $m = 2$ **f** $m = 0$
   g undefined
   h $m = \frac{1}{16}$

6 a $m = 3, c = -4$
   b $m = -1, c = -1$
   c $m = -\frac{1}{2}, c = 5$
   d $m = 1, c = 0$

e $m = \frac{1}{2}, c = \frac{1}{4}$

f $m = \frac{4}{5}, c = -2$

g m is undefined, $c = 7$

h $m = -3, c = 0$

i $m = -\frac{1}{3}, c = -\frac{14}{3}$

j $m = -1, c = -4$

k $m = 1, c = -4$

l $m = -2, c = 5$

m $m = 2, c = -20$

7 a $y = -x$ **b** $y = \frac{1}{2}x$

   c $y = 2.5$ **d** $y = -2x - 1$

   e $y = \frac{1}{2}x - 1$ **f** $y = 2x + 1$

   g $x = 2$ **h** $y = -\frac{1}{3}x + 2$

   i $y = -2x$ **j** $y = x + 4$

   k $y = 3x - 2$ **l** $y = x - 3$

Exercise 10.2

1 a $x^2 + 5x + 6$ **b** $x^2 - x - 6$

   c $x^2 + 12x + 35$ **d** $x^2 + 2x - 35$

   e $x^2 - 4x + 3$ **f** $2x^2 + x - 1$

   g $y^2 - 9y + 14$ **h** $6x^2 - 7xy + 2y^2$

   i $2x^4 - x^2 - 3$ **j** $x^2 + x - 132$

   k $1 - \frac{1}{4}x^2$ **l** $-3x^2 + 11x - 6$

   m $-12x^2 + 14x - 4$

2 a $x^2 + 8x + 16$ **b** $x^2 - 6x + 9$

   c $x^2 + 10x + 25$ **d** $y^2 - 4y + 4$

   e $x^2 + 2xy + y^2$ **f** $4x^2 - 4xy + y^2$

3 a Length $x + 40$; breadth $x - 40$

   b $A = x^2 - 1600$

   c 1600 cm^2

Mixed exercise

1 a $y = \frac{1}{2}x$

x	−1	0	2	3
y	−0.5	0	1	1.5

b $y = -\frac{1}{2}x + 3$

x	−1	0	2	3
y	3.5	3	2	1.5

c $y = 2$

x	−1	0	2	3
y	2	2	2	2

d $y - 2x - 4 = 0$

x	−1	0	2	3
y	2	4	8	10

2 a $m = -2, c = -1$

   b $m = 1, c = -6$

   c $m = 1, c = 8$

   d $m = 0, c = -\frac{1}{2}$

   e $m = -\frac{2}{3}, c = 2$

   f $m = -1, c = 0$

3 a $y = x - 3$ **b** $y = -\frac{2}{3}x + \frac{1}{2}$

   c $y = -x - 2$ **d** $y = -\frac{4}{5}x - 3$

   e $y = 2x - 3$ **f** $y = -x + 1$

   g $y = 2$ **h** $x = -4$

4 A 0, B 1, C 2, D 1, E 4

5 a $y = -2x - 6$ **b** $y = 7$

   c $y = \frac{4}{3}x + 4$ **d** $x = -10$

   e $y = -x$ **f** $y = -3$

6 a

t	0	2	4	6
D	0	14	28	42

b

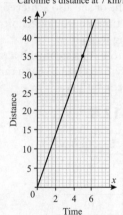

Caroline's distance at 7 km/h

   c $y = 7x$ **d** 7

   e i 3 hours   **ii** 1 h 26 min

     iii 43 min

   f i 21 km   **ii** 17.5 km

     iii 5.25 km

   g 7 hours

7 a $x^2 + 10x - 24$ **b** $x^2 - 3x - 40$

   c $4x^2 + 18x + 20$

   d $4x^2 + 12x + 9$

8 a 14, 48 i.e.

    $(x + 6)(x + 8) = x^2 + 14x + 48$

   b 4, 24 i.e.

    $(x + 4)(x + 6) = x^2 + 10x + 24$

   c 2, 2, 14 i.e.

    $(2x + 2)(2x + 7) = 4x^2 + 18x + 14$

Chapter 11

Exercise 11.1 A

1 a 5 cm   **b** 17 cm

   c 12 mm   **d** 10 cm

   e 1.09 cm   **f** 0.45 cm

   g 8.49 cm   **h** 6.11 cm

2 a 55.68 mm   **b** 14.36 cm

   c 5.29 cm   **d** 10.91 mm

   e 9.85 cm   **f** 9.33 cm

3 a no   **b** yes   **c** no

   d yes

Exercise 11.1 B

1 20 mm

2 44 cm

3 height = 86.60 mm, area = 4330.13 mm²

4 13 m and 15 m

5 0.7 m

Exercise 11.2

1 a 2.24 cm   **b** 6 mm

   c 7.5 mm   **d** 6.4 cm

   e $y = 6.67$ cm, $z = 4.8$ cm

   f $x = 5.59$ cm, $y = 13.6$ cm

   g $x = 9$ cm, $y = 24$ cm

   h $x = 50$ cm, $y = 20$ cm

2 angle ABC = angle ADE (corr angle are equal)

angle ACB = angle AED (corr angle are equal)

angle A = angle A (common)

∴ triangle ABC is similar to triangle ADE

3 25.5 m

Exercise 11.3

1 A, C, F and G are congruent.

2 Only 4 are possible.

Mixed exercise

1 a sketch   **b** 130 m

2 $10^2 = 6^2 + 8^2$ ∴ triangle ABC is right-angled (converse Pythagoras)

3 $P = 2250$ mm

4 a $x = 3.5$ cm   **b** $x = 63°, y = 87°$

   c $x = 12$ cm

5 *a*, *b* and *d*

6 5.61 m

7 a

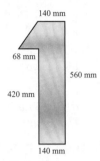

140 mm

68 mm

560 mm

420 mm

140 mm

b 156 mm

Chapter 12
Exercise 12.1

1

	a	b	c	d	e	f
mean	6.14	27.44	13.08	5	4.89	5.22
median	6	27	13	5	5	5
mode	6	27 and 38	12	no mode	4	6

2 a iii and vi
   b sensible answer from student, e.g. different sets can still add up to the same total as another set. If divided by the same number they will have the same mean.

3 255

4 15

5 Need to know how many cows there are to work out mean litres of milk produced per cow.

6 a 40   **b** 111   **c** 2.78   **d** 1

7 a $20.40   **b** $6   **c** $10
   d 2 (only the category B workers)
   e The mean is between $20 and $40 so the statement is true.

8 a 32
   b 38
   c 38.5

Exercise 12.2

1 a mean = 4.3, median = 5, mode = 2 and 5.
   The data is bimodal and the lower mode (2) is not representative of the data.

b mean = 3.15, median = 2, mode = 2.
   The mean is not representative of the data because it is too high. This is because there are some values in the data set that are much higher than the others. (This gives a big range, and when the range is big, the mean is generally not representative.)
   c mean = 17.67, median = 17, no mode.
   There is no mode, so this cannot be representative of the data. The mean and median are similar, so they are both representative of the data.

2 a mean = 12.8, median = 15, mode = 17, range = 19
   b mode too high, mean not reliable as range is large

3 a Runner B has the faster mean time; he or she also achieved the faster time, so would technically be beating Runner A.
   b A is more consistent with a range of only 2 seconds (B has a range of 3.8 seconds).

Exercise 12.3

1

Score	Frequency
0	6
1	6
2	10
3	11
4	5
5	1
6	1
Total	40

a 2.25   **b** 3   **c** 2
d 6

2

Data set	A	B	C
mean	3.5	46.14	4.12
median	3	40	4.5
mode	3 and 5	40	6.5

Mixed exercise

1 a mean 6.4, median 6, mode 6, range 6
   b mean 2.6, median 2, mode 2, range 5
   c mean 13.8, median 12.8, no mode, range 11.9

2 a 19   **b** 9 and 10   **c** 5.66

3 C – although B's mean is bigger it has a larger range. C's smaller range suggests that its mean is probably more representative.

4 a 4.82 cm³   **b** 5 cm³   **c** 5 cm³

Chapter 13
Exercise 13.1

1 student's own diagrams

2 a 2600 m   **b** 230 mm
   c 820 cm   **d** 2450.809 km
   e 20 mm   **f** 0.157 m

3 a 9080 g   **b** 49340 g
   c 500 g   **d** 0.068 kg
   e 0.0152 kg   **f** 2.3 tonne

4 a 19 km   100 m
   b 9015 cm   15 cm
   c 435 mm   2 mm
   d 492 cm   63 cm
   e 635 m   35 m
   f 580500 cm   500 cm

5 a 1200 mm²   **b** 900 mm²
   c 16420 mm²   **d** 370000 m²
   e 0.009441 km²   **f** 423000 mm²

6 a 69000 mm³
   b 19000 mm³
   c 30040 mm³
   d 4815000 cm³
   e 0.103 cm³
   f 0.0000469 m³

7 220 m

8 110 cm

9 42 cm

10 88 (round down as you cannot have part of a box)

Exercise 13.2

1

Name	Time in	Time out	Lunch	(a) Hours worked	(b) Daily earnings
Dawoot	$\frac{1}{4}$ past 9	Half past five	$\frac{3}{4}$ hour	$7\frac{1}{2}$ hours	$55.88
Nadira	8:17 a.m.	5:30 p.m.	$\frac{1}{2}$ hour	8 h 43 min	$64.94
John	08:23	17:50	45 min	8 h 42 min	$64.82
Robyn	7:22 a.m.	4:30 p.m.	1 hour	8 h 8 min	$60.59
Mari	08:08	18:30	45 min	9 h 37 min	$71.64

2 6 h 25 min

3 20 min

4 a 5 h 47 min   **b** 11 h 26 min
   c 12 h 12 min   **d** 14 h 30 min

5 a 09:00   **b** 1 hour   **c** 09:30
   d 30 minutes

   e It would arrive late at Peron Place at 10:54 and at Marquez Lane at 11:19.

Exercise 13.3

1 The upper bound is 'inexact' so 42.5 in table means < 42.5

	Upper bound	Lower bound
a	42.5	41.5
b	13325.5	13324.5
c	450	350
d	12.245	12.235
e	11.495	11.485
f	2.55	2.45
g	395	385
h	1.1325	1.1315

2 a $71.5 \leqslant h < 72.5$
   b Yes, it is less than 72.5 (although it would be impossible to measure to that accuracy).

Exercise 13.4

1 a 1 unit = 100000 rupiah

b i 250000
   ii 500000
   iii 2500000
c i Aus$80
   ii Aus$640

2 a Temperature in degrees C against temperature in degrees F
   b i 32 °F   **ii** 50 °F
     iii 220 °F
   c oven could be marked in Fahrenheit, but of course she could also have experienced a power failure or other practical problem
   d Fahrenheit scale as 50 °C is hot, not cold

3 a 9 kg   **b** 45 kg
   c i 20 kg   **ii** 35 kg
     iii 145 lb

Exercise 13.5

1 a i US$1 = ¥76.16
     ii £1 = NZ$1.99
     iii €1 = IR69.10
     iv Can$1 = €0.71
     v ¥1 = £0.01
     vi R1 = US$0.12
   b i 2490.50   **ii** 41460
     iii 7540.15
   c i 9139.20   **ii** 52820
     iii 145632

Mixed exercise

1 a 2700 m   **b** 690 mm
   c 6000 kg   **d** 0.0235 kg
   e 263000 mg   **f** 29250 ml
   g 0.24 l   **h** 1000 mm²
   i 0.006428 km²   **j** 7900000 cm³
   k 29000000 m³   **l** 0.168 cm³

2 23 min 45 s

3 2 h 19 min 55 s

4 $1.615 \,\text{m} \leqslant h < 1.625 \,\text{m}$

5 a No, that is lower than the lower bound of 45
   b Yes, that is within the bounds

6 a conversion graph showing litres against gallons (conversion factor)
   b i 45 l   **ii** 112.5 l
   c i 3.33 gallons   **ii** 26.67 gallons
   d i 48.3 km/g and 67.62 km/g
     ii 10.62 km/l and 14.87 km/l

7 €892.06

8 a US$1 = IR49.81   **b** 99620
   c US$249.95

9 £4239.13

Chapter 14
Exercise 14.1

1 a

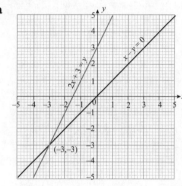

$x = -3, y = -3$

b

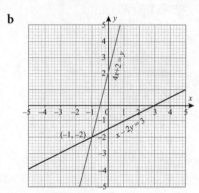

$x = -1, y = -2$

c

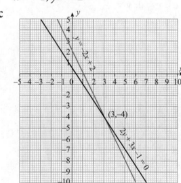

$x = 3, y = -4$

d

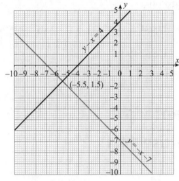

$x = -5.5, y = -1.5$

e

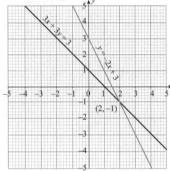

$x = 2, y = -1$

2 a i $y = -x + 4$
    ii $2y = 3x + 12$
    iii $y = -4x - 2$
    iv $y = x$
    v $y = -2$
    vi $y = x - 4$
 b i $(-2, 6)$ **ii** $(-2, -2)$
    iii $(4, 0)$

3 a $x = 4, y = 2$
 b $x = -1, y = 2$
 c $x = 0, y = 4$
 d $x = 3, y = 1$

4 a $x = 6, y = -1$
 b $x = 1, y = 2$
 c $x = 18, y = -8$
 d $x = 1, y = 1\frac{1}{3}$
 e $x = 3, y = -1$
 f $x = 3, y = 7$

5 a $x = 2, y = 1$
 b $x = 2, y = 2$
 c $x = 2, y = -1$
 d $x = 3, y = 2$
 e $x = 3, y = 2.5$
 f $x = 4, y = 2$

g $x = 5, y = 3$
h $x = 0.5, y = -0.5$
i $x = -9, y = -2$

6 a chocolate bar costs \$1.20 and a box of gums \$0.75

7 number of students is 7

8 6 quarters and 6 dimes

Mixed exercise

1 $x = 2$ and $y = -5$

2 $x = -2$ and $y = 5$

3 \$5000 at 5% and \$10000 at 8%

4 Solve $5L - 2B = 12$ and $2L + 2B = 9$ simultaneously.
$L = 3$ metres and $B = 1.5$ metres

5 a $2x + 5y = 30$ and $x - 5y = 10$
 b $x = 13\frac{1}{3}$ and $y = \frac{2}{3}$
 c $2x + 5y = 30$
    $x - 5y = 10$
    $3x = 40$
    $x = 13.33 \ldots$
    $y = 0.66 \ldots$

Chapter 15

Exercise 15.1

1 a length $= 10$ cm, width $= 7$ cm
 b length $= 14.4$ cm, width $= 7$ cm

2 a length $= 9.14$ cm, width $= 5.5$ cm

 b Yes. The length of the mini pitch = width of standard pitch and $2 \times$ width of mini pitch < length of standard pitch. It is possible to have two mini pitches on a standard pitch so, with three standard pitches, up to six matches could take place at the same time.

3 a $\frac{1}{200}$ or $\frac{1}{150}$
 b **i** and **ii** diagram drawn using student's scale including x for net posts

4 a student's scale drawing – diagonal distance $= 11.3$ m
 b using Pythagoras' theorem

Exercise 15.2

1 a 090°
 b 225°
 c 315°

2 a 250°   **b** 310°   **c** 135°

3 student's drawing
 a 223°   **b** 065°   **c** 11 km
 d 13 km

Exercise 15.3

1

	a	b	c	d
hypotenuse	c	z	f	q
opp(A)	a	y	g	p
adj(A)	b	x	e	r

2 a opp(30°) $= x$ cm
    adj(60°) $= x$ cm
    opp(60°) $=$ adj(30°) $= y$ cm
 b adj(40°) $= q$ cm
    opp(50°) $= q$ cm
    opp(40°) $=$ adj(50°) $= p$ cm

3 a 0.65   **b** 1.43   **c** 5.14
 d 0.41   **e** 0

4 a $\tan A = \frac{3}{4}$ **b** $\tan x = \frac{2}{3}, \tan y = \frac{3}{2}$
 c $\tan 55° = \frac{1}{d}, \tan B = d$
 d $\tan y = \frac{5}{12}$, angle $X = (90 - y)°, \tan X = \frac{12}{5}$
 e $AC = 2$ cm, $\tan B = \frac{4}{3}, \tan C = \frac{3}{4}$

5 a $x = 1.40$ cm
 b $y = 19.29$ m
 c $c = 3.32$ cm
 d $a = 13$ m
 e $x = 35.70$ cm

6 a 26.6°   **b** 40.9°   **c** 51.3°
 d 85.2°   **e** 14.0°   **f** 40.9°
 g 79.7°   **h** 44.1°

7 a 16°   **b** 46°   **c** 49°
 d 23°   **e** 38°

8 a hyp $= y$, adj$(\theta) = z$, $\cos\theta = \frac{z}{y}$
 b hyp $= c$, adj$(\theta) = b$, $\cos\theta = \frac{b}{c}$
 c hyp $= c$, adj$(\theta) = a$, $\cos\theta = \frac{a}{c}$
 d hyp $= p$, adj$(\theta) = r$, $\cos\theta = \frac{r}{p}$
 e hyp $= x$, adj$(\theta) = z$, $\cos\theta = \frac{z}{x}$

9 a $\sin A = \frac{7}{13}, \cos A = \frac{12}{13}, \tan A = \frac{7}{12}$

b $\sin B = \frac{5}{11}, \cos B = \frac{19.6}{22}, \tan B = \frac{10}{19.6}$

c $\sin C = \frac{3}{5}, \cos C = \frac{4}{5}, \tan C = \frac{3}{4}$

d $\sin D = \frac{63}{65}, \cos D = \frac{16}{65}, \tan D = \frac{63}{16}$

e $\sin E = \frac{84}{85}, \cos E = \frac{13}{85}, \tan E = \frac{84}{13}$

10 a 45° **b** 64° **c** 57°
d 60° **e** 30° **f** 27°

11 4.86 m

Mixed exercise

1 a $x = 37.6°$ **b** $x = 44.0°$

2 53.5°, 90°

Chapter 16

1 a E **b** C **c** A
d D **e** B

2 a student's own line (line should go close to (160, 4.5) and (170, 5.5)) answers (b) and (c) depend on student's best fit line
b ≈ 4.75 m
c between 175 and 180 cm
d fairly strongly positive
e taller athletes can jump further

Mixed exercise

1 a the number of accidents for different speeds
b average speed
answers to (c) depend on student's best fit line
c i ≈ 35 accidents
ii < 40 km/h
d strong positive
e there are more accidents when vehicles are travelling at a higher average speed

2 a there a strong negative correlation at first, but this becomes weaker as the cars get older

b 0–2 years
c it stabilises around the $6000 level
d 2–3 years
e 5–8 thousand dollars

Chapter 17
Exercise 17.1

1 $19.26

2 $25560

3 a $930.75 **b** $1083.75
c $765 **d** $1179.38

4 $1203.40

5 $542.75

6 a $625 **b** $25 **c** $506.50

Exercise 17.2

1 a $7.50 **b** $160 **c** $210
d $448 **e** $343.75

2 5 years

3 2.8%

4 $2800 more

5 $2281 more

6 a $7.50 **b** $187.73
c $225.75 **d** $574.55
e $346.08

7 $562.75

8 $27085.85

Exercise 17.3

1 a $100 **b** $200 **c** $340
d $900

2 $300

3 $500

4 $64.41

5 a $179.10
b $40.04
c $963.90

Mixed exercise

1 a 12 h **b** 40 h **c** $25\frac{1}{2}$ h

2 a $1190 **b** $1386 **c** $1232

3 a $62808 **b** $4149.02

4 a

Years	Simple interest	Compound interest
1	300	300
2	600	609
3	900	927.27
4	1200	1125.09
5	1500	1592.74
6	1800	1940.52
7	2100	2298.74
8	2400	2667.70

b $92.74
c student's own graph; a comment such as, the amount of compound interest increases faster than the simple interest

5 $862.50

6 $3360

7 a $1335, $2225
b $1950, $3250
c $18000, $30000

8 a $4818 **b** 120%

9 $425

10 $211.20

11 $43.36 (each)

12 $204

Chapter 18
Exercise 18.1

1

	x	−3	−2	−1	0	1	2	3
a	$y = -x^2 + 2$	−7	−2	1	2	1	−2	−7
b	$y = x^2 - 3$	6	1	−2	−3	−2	1	6
c	$y = -x^2 - 2$	−11	−6	−3	−2	−3	−6	−11
d	$y = -x^2 - 3$	−12	−7	−4	−3	−4	−7	−12
e	$y = x^2 + \frac{1}{2}$	9.5	4.5	1.5	0.5	1.5	4.5	9.5

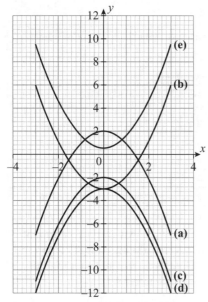

2 **a** $y = x^2 + 3$ **b** $y = x^2 + 2$
   c $y = x^2$ **d** $y = -x^2 + 3$
   e $y = -x^2 - 4$

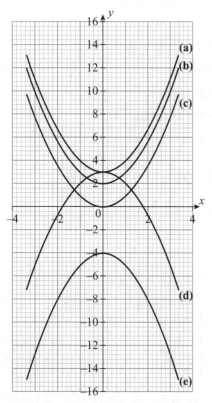

3 **a**

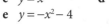

x	−2	−1	0	1	2	3	4	5
$y = x^2 - 3x + 2$	12	6	2	0	0	2	6	12

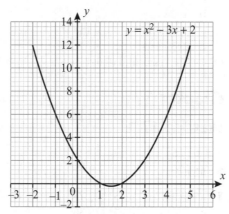

b

x	−3	−2	−1	0	1	2	3
$y = x^2 - 2x - 1$	14	7	2	−1	−2	−1	2

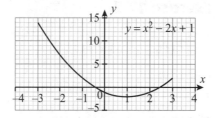

c

x	−2	−1	0	1	2	3	4	5	6
$y = -x^2 + 4x + 1$	−11	−4	1	4	5	4	1	−4	−11

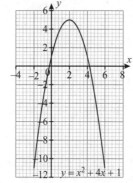

4 **a**

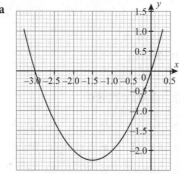

$y = x^2 + 3x$

b

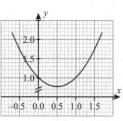

$y = x^2 - x + 1$

c

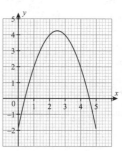

$y = -x^2 + 5x - 2$

5 **a** 8 m   **b** 2 seconds
   c 6 m
   d just short of 4 seconds
   e 3 seconds

Exercise 18.2

1 **a**

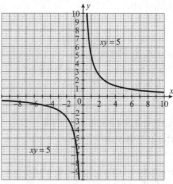

b

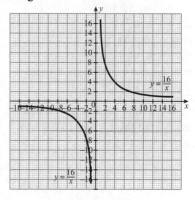

c

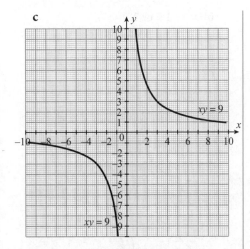

d

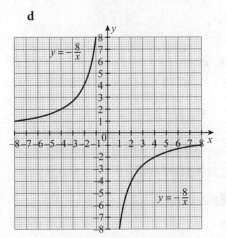

e

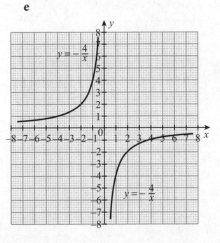

2 a

length	1	2	3	4	6	8	12	24
width	24	12	8	6	4	3	2	1

b

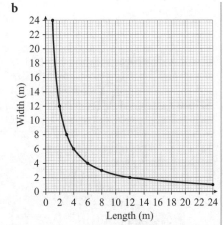

c the curve represents all the possible measurements for the rectangle with an area of 24 m²

d ≈ 3.4 m

Exercise 18.3

1 a −2 or 3 **b** −1 or 2

c −3 or 4

2 a

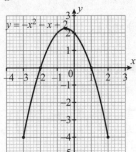

b i −2 or 1

ii ≈ −1.6 or 0.6

iii ≈ −2.6 or 1.6

3 a

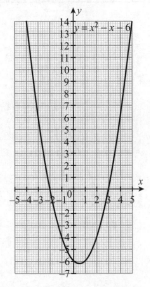

b i 0 or 1

ii −2 or 3

iii −3 or 4

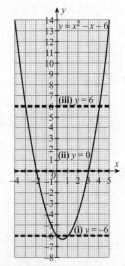

Exercise 18.4

1 a

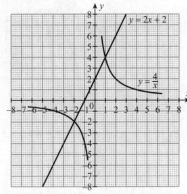

(1, 4) and (−2, −2)

b

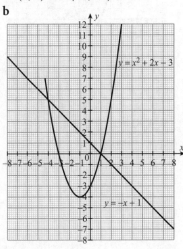

(−4, 5) and (1, 0)

c

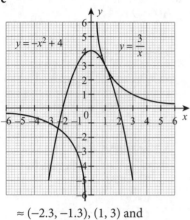

$y = -x^2 + 4$ $y = \dfrac{3}{x}$

$\approx (-2.3, -1.3)$, $(1, 3)$ and $(1.3, 2.3)$

2 a

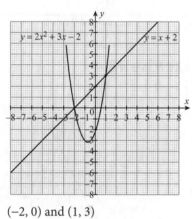

$y = 2x^2 + 3x - 2$ $y = x + 2$

$(-2, 0)$ and $(1, 3)$

b

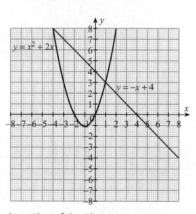

$y = x^2 + 2x$ $y = -x + 4$

$(-4, 8)$ and $(1, 3)$

c

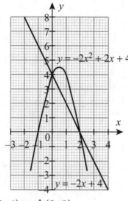

$y = -2x^2 + 2x + 4$ $y = -2x + 4$

$(0, 4)$ and $(2, 0)$

d

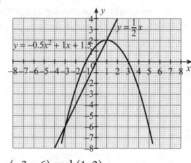

$y = -0.5x^2 + 1x + 1.5$ $y = \tfrac{1}{2}x$

$(-3, -6)$ and $(1, 2)$

Mixed exercise

1 a

x	-3	-2	-1	0	1	2	3	4
$y = x^2 - 8$	1	-4	-7	-8	-7	-4	1	8

x	-3	-2	-1	0	1	2	3	4
$y = 2x - 3$	-9	-7	-5	-3	-1	1	3	5

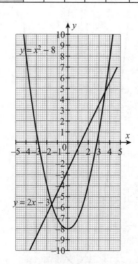

$y = x^2 - 8$ $y = 2x - 3$

b $x \approx -1.5$ or 3.5

c minimum value $= -8$

2 a $y = -\dfrac{4}{x}$ **b** $y = x$

c

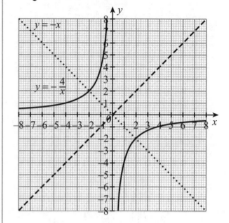

$y = -x$ $y = -\dfrac{4}{x}$

3 a $y = -x$

b $y = -7$

c $y = -x^2$

d $y = -\dfrac{1}{x}$

e $y = -\dfrac{1}{x} + 4$

Chapter 19

Exercise 19.1

1 a

A   B

C   D

E   F

G

H has no line symmetry

b A = 0, B = 3, C = 4, D = 4, E = 5, F = 2, G = 2, H = 2

2 a 2, student's diagram
b 2

3 student's own diagrams but as an example:

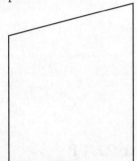

Exercise 19.2

1 100°

2 54°

3 w = 90°, tangent meets radius
x = 53°, angles on a straight line
y = 90°, angle in a semi-circle
z = 53°, angles in a triangle

Mixed exercise

1 a i   **ii** none

b i   **ii** none

c i   **ii** four

d i   **ii** eight

e i   **ii** none

2 a = b = 28°, c = 56°, d = e = 34°

Chapter 20
Exercise 20.1

1 a

English exam marks

Maths exam marks

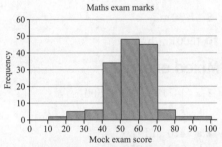

b 51–60   **c** 51–60
d students to compare based on histograms, but possible comments are: The modal value for both subjects is the same but the number in the English mode is higher than the Maths. Maths has more students scoring between 40 and 70 marks. Maths had more students scoring more than 90 marks and fewer scoring less than 20.

2 a bars are touching, scale on horizontal axis is continuous, vertical axis shows frequency
b 55   **c** 315   **d** 29–31
e scale does not start from 0

Mixed exercise

1 a

Heights of trees

b 19   **c** 6–8 metres

2 a

Masses of students

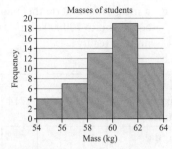

b 60–62 kg
c 7.4%
d 10 kg

Chapter 21
Exercise 21.1

1 a 4:5   **b** 3:4   **c** 6:1
d 5:14   **e** 9:40   **f** 7:8
g 1:5   **h** 1:20   **i** 1:4
j 6:5   **k** 1:15

2 a x = 9   **b** x = 4
c x = 16   **d** x = 3
e x = 4   **f** x = 1.14
g x = 1.875   **h** x = 2.67
i x = 7   **j** x = 13.33

3 Nesta = $7200, Tyson = $4800

4 100 and 250

5 60 cm and 100 cm

6 a 20 ml oil and 30 ml vinegar
b 240 ml oil and 360 ml vinegar
c 300 ml oil and 450 ml vinegar

7 60°, 30° and 90°

8 810 mg

Exercise 21.2 A

1 a 1:2.25   **b** 1:3.25
c 1:1.8

2 a 1.5:1   **b** 5:1
c 5:1

Exercise 21.2 B

1 240 km

2 30 m

3 a 5 cm
b 3.5 cm

4 a it means one unit on the map is equivalent to 700000 of the same units in reality

b

Map distance (mm)	10	71	50	80	1714	2143
Actual distance (km)	7	50	35	56	1200	1500

5 a 4:1   **b** 14.8 cm
c 120 mm or 12 cm

Exercise 21.3

1 25.6 l

2 11.5 km/l

3 a 78.4 km/h
b 520 km/h
c 240 km/h

4 a 5 h   **b** 9 h 28 min
c 40 h   **d** 4.29 min

5 a 150 km   **b** 300 km
c 3.75 km   **d** 18 km

6 $\frac{14\,500}{725} = 20 \text{ g/cm}^3$

Exercise 21.4

1 a i 100 km
ii 200 km
iii 300 km
b 100 km/h
c vehicle stopped
d 250 km
e 125 km/h

2 a 2 hours
b 190 min = 3 h 10 min
c 120 km/h
d i 120 km
ii 80 km
e 48 km/h
f 40 min
g 50 min
h 53.3 − 48 = 5.3 km/h
i Pam 12 noon, Dabilo 11:30 a.m.

Exercise 21.5

1 a Yes, $\frac{A}{B} = \frac{1}{150}$
b No, $\frac{8}{15}$ is not $= \frac{1}{2}$
c Yes, $\frac{A}{B} = \frac{10}{1}$

2 a $175   **b** $250

3 $12.50

4 60 m

5 a 75 km   **b** 375 km
c 3 h 20 min

6 a 15 litres   **b** 540 km

7 a inversely proportional
b i $2\frac{1}{2}$ days
ii $\frac{1}{2}$ day

8 a 12 days   **b** 5 days

9 5 h 30 min

10 1200 km/h

Mixed exercise

1 a 14:19   **b** 1:500
c 1:8

2 a 420 and 180
b 350 and 250
c 210 and 390
d 300 and 300

3 a 1 spadeful
b 0.5 bags
c 0.375 wheelbarrows full

4 a 90 mm, 150 mm and 120 mm
b Yes, $(150)^2 = (90)^2 + (120)^2$

5 5 cm

6 1:50

7 a 10.10 m/s
b 36.36 km/h

8 a i 85 km
ii 382.5 km
iii 21.25 km
b i 0.35 h
ii 4.7 h
iii 1.18 h

9 a 150 km
b after 2 hours for 1 hour
c 100 km/h
d 100 km/h
e 500 km

10 4.5 min

11 187.5 g

Chapter 22

Exercise 22.1 A

1 9

2 26

3 134

4 8

5 6

6 7 and 2

7 2

8 40 and 60

Exercise 22.1 B

1 a $x - 4$
b $P = 4x - 8$
c $A = x^2 - 4x$

2 a $S = 5x + 2$
b $M = \frac{5x + 2}{3}$

3 a $x + 1, x + 2$
b $S = 3x + 3$

4 a $x + 2$ **b** $x - 3$
c $S = 3x - 1$

Exercise 22.1 C

1 14

2 9 cm

3 80 silver cars, 8 red cars

4 father = 35, mother = 33 and Nadira = 10

5 breadth = 13 cm, length = 39 cm

6 a $2x + 5 = 2 - x$
b $x = -1$

7 a $P = 3x + 12$
b i 11 cm, 15 cm and 19 cm
ii 3.75 cm, 7.75 cm and 11.75 cm

Mixed exercise

1 10

2 4

3 4

4 Nathi has $67 and Cedric has $83

5 55

6 $40 and $20

7 a $P = 4x + 2$
  b length = 27 mm, width = 22 mm

Chapter 23

Exercise 23.1 A

1

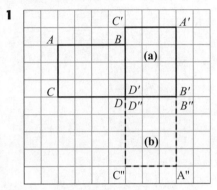

2

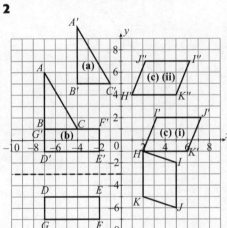

3

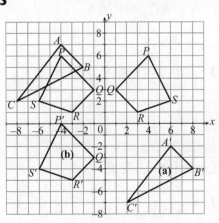

4 A: $y = 5$
  B: $x = 0$
  C: $y = -1.5$
  D: $x = -6$

5

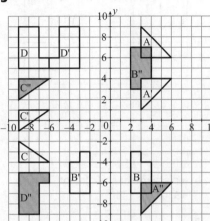

6 possible answers are:

for *ABC*: rotate 90° anticlockwise about *B* then reflect in the line $x = -6$

for *MNOP*: rotate 90° anticlockwise about (2, 1) then reflect in the line $x = 5$

Exercise 23.1 B

1 A: centre (0, 2), scale factor 2
  B: centre (1, 0), scale factor 2
  C: centre (−4, −7), scale factor 2
  D: centre (9, −5), scale factor $\frac{1}{4}$

2
a i

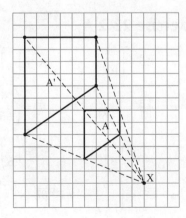

ii

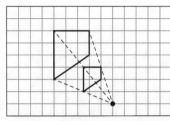

b i

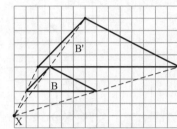

ii

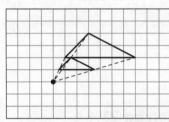

c i

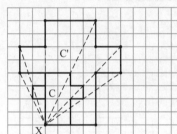

ii

d i

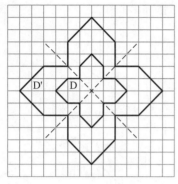

ii

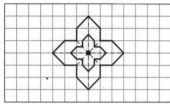

Exercise 23.1 C

1 a

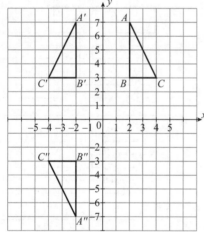

b rotation 180° about (0, 0)

2 a

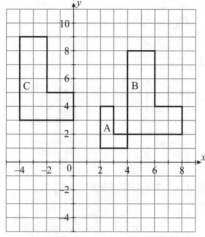

b enlargement scale factor 2, using (5, −1) as centre

3 a

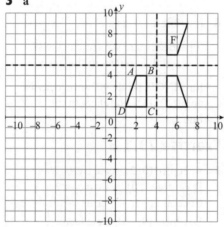

b rotation 180° about (4, 5)

Exercise 23.2 A

1 a $\overrightarrow{AB} = \begin{pmatrix} 5 \\ 0 \end{pmatrix}$ **b** $\overrightarrow{BC} = \begin{pmatrix} 4 \\ 0 \end{pmatrix}$

c $\overrightarrow{AE} = \begin{pmatrix} 0 \\ -6 \end{pmatrix}$ **d** $\overrightarrow{BD} = \begin{pmatrix} -1 \\ -6 \end{pmatrix}$

e $\overrightarrow{DB} = \begin{pmatrix} 1 \\ 6 \end{pmatrix}$ **f** $\overrightarrow{EC} = \begin{pmatrix} 9 \\ 6 \end{pmatrix}$

g $\overrightarrow{CD} = \begin{pmatrix} -5 \\ -6 \end{pmatrix}$ **h** $\overrightarrow{BE} = \begin{pmatrix} -5 \\ -6 \end{pmatrix}$

i they are equal

j $\begin{pmatrix} 9 \\ 0 \end{pmatrix}$ **k** $\begin{pmatrix} -5 \\ -6 \end{pmatrix}$

l Yes

2 a

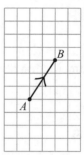

b

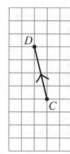

c

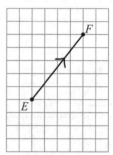

d

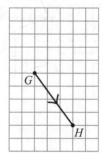

3 A $\begin{pmatrix} 8 \\ 1 \end{pmatrix}$ B $\begin{pmatrix} 2 \\ 3 \end{pmatrix}$ C $\begin{pmatrix} 4 \\ -3 \end{pmatrix}$

    D $\begin{pmatrix} -3 \\ -3 \end{pmatrix}$ E $\begin{pmatrix} 9 \\ 3 \end{pmatrix}$

Exercise 23.2 B

1 a $\begin{pmatrix} -8 \\ 16 \end{pmatrix}$ **b** $\begin{pmatrix} 2 \\ 6 \end{pmatrix}$ **c** $\begin{pmatrix} 0 \\ 12 \end{pmatrix}$

    d $\begin{pmatrix} -1 \\ 7 \end{pmatrix}$ **e** $\begin{pmatrix} -2 \\ 1 \end{pmatrix}$ **f** $\begin{pmatrix} -1 \\ 4 \end{pmatrix}$

g $\begin{pmatrix} -4 \\ 18 \end{pmatrix}$ **h** $\begin{pmatrix} -8 \\ 22 \end{pmatrix}$ **i** $\begin{pmatrix} 0 \\ -20 \end{pmatrix}$

j $\begin{pmatrix} 10 \\ -16 \end{pmatrix}$

2 a $-\mathbf{a}$ **b** $2\mathbf{b}$ **c** $-\mathbf{a}+\mathbf{c}$
  d $2\mathbf{c}$ **e** $2\mathbf{b}$ **f** $2\mathbf{c}$
  g $\mathbf{b}$ **h** $-\mathbf{c}$ **i** $-\mathbf{a}+\mathbf{c}$
  j $\dfrac{\mathbf{b}}{2}+3\mathbf{c}$

Mixed exercise

1 a i reflect in the line $x=-1$

    ii rotate 90° clockwise about the origin

    iii reflect in the line $y=-1$

  b i rotate 90° anticlockwise about $(0, 0)$ then translate $\begin{pmatrix} -2 \\ -1 \end{pmatrix}$

    ii reflect in the line $y=-1$ then translate $\begin{pmatrix} -8 \\ 0 \end{pmatrix}$

    iii rotate 180° about origin then translate $\begin{pmatrix} 6 \\ 0 \end{pmatrix}$

    iv reflect in the line $x=0$ (y-axis) then translate $\begin{pmatrix} 0 \\ -2 \end{pmatrix}$

2

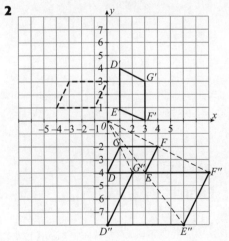

3

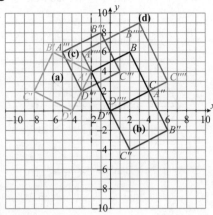

a B′ $(-6, -6)$ **b** B′ $(6, -2)$
c B′ $(-1, 8)$ **d** B′ $(3, 9)$

4 a i $\begin{pmatrix} 6 \\ 12 \end{pmatrix}$ **ii** $\begin{pmatrix} 0 \\ -8 \end{pmatrix}$

    iii $\begin{pmatrix} 1 \\ 10 \end{pmatrix}$ **iv** $\begin{pmatrix} 12 \\ 0 \end{pmatrix}$

  b i

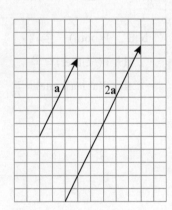

    ii

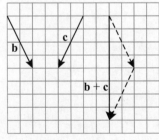

    iii

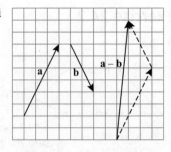

    iv

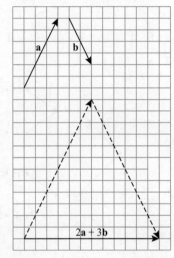

Chapter 24

Exercise 24.1

1

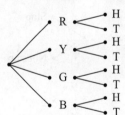

2

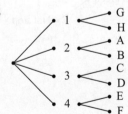

Exercise 24.2

1 a

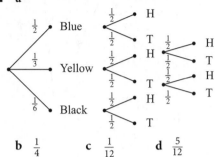

b $\frac{1}{4}$ **c** $\frac{1}{12}$ **d** $\frac{5}{12}$

2 a

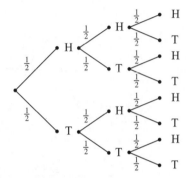

b $\frac{1}{8}$ **c** $\frac{1}{2}$

d $\frac{1}{2}$

e 0, not possible on three coin tosses

3 a

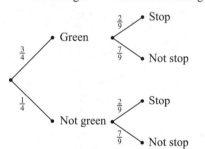

b $\frac{1}{18}$

c $\frac{7}{12}$

4 a

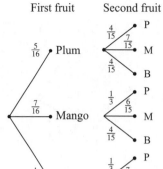

b $\frac{1}{12}$

5 a

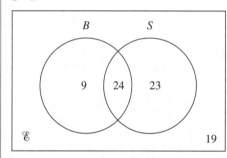

b i P(both) $= \frac{24}{75} = \frac{8}{25}$

ii P(neither) $= \frac{19}{75}$

iii P(at least one) $= \frac{56}{75}$

Mixed exercise

1 a & b

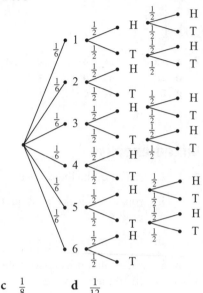

c $\frac{1}{8}$ **d** $\frac{1}{12}$

2 a

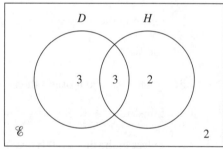

b i $\frac{3}{10}$ **ii** $\frac{3}{10}$ **iii** $\frac{4}{5}$

c 20% chance of getting neither.